Wicca Spells

An Introductory Guide to Candle, Crystal, Herbal and Moon Magic to Start your Enchanted Endeavors

Contents

Introduction

As we continue to grow, we also seek to understand ourselves better. Sometimes we look for answers in uncommon places. Often we find that these new perspectives spark a change within us. Always, we learn something new.

Wicca is a space that preserved the wisdom of the ancients. This book will share with you what it really is about. It will help you design a life full of wonder. A love for nature. And a desire to embrace all facets of yourself.

This book contains proven steps and strategies on how to perform Wiccan spells for various purposes. It contains everything you need to know to get you started in performing spells. You can find lots of spells that vary in complexity for different purposes in this book.

Enjoy this journey through Wicca. Whether you really are a beginner, or an old witch who wants to rekindle the flame, this book is for you.

Chapter 1: The Basics

If your spiritual search has led you to Wicca, you are not alone. It is understandable if you are confused on how to start on your new path. Maybe, you have no idea on how you can be a full-fledged Wiccan. With dedication and faith, you will learn everything you need to know.

In the simplest sense, Wicca is now understood as a polytheistic Earth-based religion. Many witches practice it, but not all of them do. Moreover, many people practice it but not all of them are witches.

There are many misconceptions surrounding Wicca. One of which is that becoming a Wiccan will enable you to become supernatural. Or that it is only meant for "special" people with super powers. No, that is not Wiccan at all.

Wiccans aim to live in harmony with Nature. They do not have to become witches – practice magick – to show reverence to Nature and to live in the now.

Wiccans believe that life here on Earth is meant to pursue knowledge. It is also meant to understand both painful and pleasurable experiences. Wiccans concentrate on what it means to be a part of this Earth. They do not think that they are here just to wait for death and the hereafter reward or punishment.

Wicca is a religion that you should not follow to rebel against your family or society, or to be "cool." Neither should you consider being Wiccan only to learn how to put spells on people. It does not work that way.

Learning how to do magick and perform spells is part of being Wiccan. But, as with everything else in life, you have to be responsible for your actions. Let's explore the most important principles first.

Wicca's Two Major Rules

Wicca is a very open religion. It is not staunch. Thus, there aren't too many regulations and rules. But, there are two main rules that you need to learn to become a true Wiccan.

Wiccans strive to abide by these two major rules.

-An Ye Harm None, Do as Ye Will. – This is equivalent to the Christian teaching "do unto others what you want others to do to you. But, the Wiccan rule is more basic. This means if you're planning on performing your very first spell, and will bring harm or confusion to another person or yourself, you need to rethink your intentions of being a Wiccan.

A true Wiccan believes that everything and everyone has a definite purpose, and is part of the universe. Everyone is one with the goddesses and gods. Thus, you wouldn't want to bring harm to the gods or the universe, right? You don't want to harm others or yourself. After all, we're all one with the universe.

-Whatever you do will come back to you threefold. – Doesn't this remind you of Karma? It sure does, and it is very true. Whatever decisions you make, and whatever you decide to do in your life, will have a consequence. This can either be bad or good. Practicing Wicca is the same. If you put a spell on your enemy to take vengeance, all that revengeful energy and negativity will come crashing right back to you – 3x the severity of what you sent out there. You wouldn't want that, would you?

The good news is that if you are a kind-hearted and loving person, then the opposite is true. In time, you will get the kindness and love back – more than what you initially gave. But, don't start doing nice things to everyone you know for selfish reasons. The universe and Karma don't work that way!

To be a Wiccan, you must understand these two main rules by heart. You need to follow them wholeheartedly. It is also important to continue to learn. Research and read various resources on how to live the life of a Wiccan.

Performing Your First Ritual

Whether you are practicing on your own or with a coven, you may find your first Wiccan ritual somewhat terrifying. I'm sure you're anxious to know why.

Well, for one, it is something new to you. It is understandable that you worry how everything will turn out. The following questions may pop in your head:

Will I say the right words?

Will I cast the circle the right way?

Will I remember to ground and center?

Don't worry. Even if you don't do everything perfect, sometimes, there's beauty in chaos.

Before doing your very first ritual, determine if you want to go solo, and practice on your own. Or, do you want to be part of a coven (a group of practicing Wiccans)? You have better chances of finding a coven if you are living in an urban area compared to a rural community. You can search for local covens online.

When doing your first ritual as a solo Wiccan practitioner, it is best that you start with something quick and simple. You may light a candle while saying a short prayer prior to bedtime. This may be for protection or for love, or anything else. Then, perform a specific meditation as you wake up, as you watch the sun climb its way up to the sky.

A simple cleansing bath may also do. Focus on the loving and healing energies of the water that surrounds and envelops your whole body. You can connect with the different elements in an effective but simple way….and that can be your first Wiccan ritual.

Casting a Love Spell

For our first example, let's use a love spell. Learning how to cast a love spell can mean half the battle won in your quest for a new romance in your life. You will learn how to cast love spells in a more in-depth manner in succeeding chapters of this book.

Your Target

A key to learning how to cast a love spell is identifying your target. Do you want to direct a spell at a particular person to change his/her feelings for you? Or, do you want to stick with a generic attraction spell, which isn't meant for anyone in particular? It depends on the situation.

There's nothing wrong with putting out a generic spell. But, to cast a spell on a specific person to create feelings that aren't existing? That can be quite tricky, and it may bring you some trouble in the future.

If you are only putting out your need for love so the universe can grant it, then that's fine. It is the more common approach. You have better chances of finding true love this way, instead of creating it for yourself.

The Techniques

There are various elements that make up a solid love spell. These include:

-The red color, together with white and pink

-The water element or chalice

-Herbs such as rose, damiana, cloves, vanilla, dragon's blood, vervain, and mandrake

-Stones like ruby, garnet, and red jasper

-Your target's personal items, or photo

If possible, cast your spell on a Friday. This is the day dedicated to Frigga, a Norse goddess. While doing the spell, focus all your emotions and thoughts on your objective – be it a specific person or no one in particular.

If you want your spell to be open to all, though you have someone specific in mind, try not to focus any energy or thoughts on them. Let your mind be open, or you may misdirect your energy.

Just because you do not mention someone's name in the spell doesn't mean it will not head their way. Keep these things in mind when you are planning on using a spell to find love.

How to Determine if Your Spells Work

Magick is energy that anyone can create. It's not true that only extraordinary and unique people can put a spell. Anyone can cast a magick spell, and change how things are. Although some people can do it more easily, anyone, including you, can become an expert if you are willing to put in some time to practice.

Often, people come to practicing Wiccans to ask the latter to perform magick for them. This usually ends up in unsatisfactory results. It is not because the Wiccans will not try their best. But, it is because they don't have intimate associations with your issues, as well as your deep need for the spell to work.

One important factor for making your spells work depends on how you put all the materials together, as well as how you incorporate your energy. Your spells are real, and will work – if you are really serious in casting them.

Remember that once you have decided on a spell, you should commit to it. You should have no doubts on its magick. You must trust in its strength, even if your words sound a bit strange. Your spell is your way to channel the great energies of the element you have chosen. A shadow of a doubt will not make it work.

Chapter 2: Candle Spells

You can use Wiccan candle spells for almost all kinds of purposes. They are simple and easy enough to perform. Also, candles are widely available. You can quickly get familiar with these type of spells, as they are one of the most simple to perform. You'll find several spells for different purposes in this chapter.

First, let's learn some of the most important details about candle spells.

Candle Colors

Candle spells are based on similar principles and ideas to those of color therapy. Just like in color therapy, each color has a different frequency and thus, each will have unique effects.

Let's explore the effects of the most widely used colors in Wicca:

-White – White includes all colors. It is a symbol of innocence and purity. It is also the Triple Goddess' Maiden aspect. Use white for purification, healing, peace, cleansing, sincerity and truth, clarity, spirituality, joy, and wholeness. You can also use it for protection, relieving tension, repelling negative energy, and meditation help.

-Yellow – This is the color of creativity, intellect, and inspiration. Use yellow for charm and confidence, wisdom, persuasion, concentration, mental strength, memory, communication, learning, and logic. It fuels your self-esteem and personal power. It also promotes optimism and cheerfulness. You can use it to represent or invoke the air element.

-Orange – Orange energizes you, and promotes joy, success, and stimulation. Use it to attract good fortune, power, prosperity, energy building, action, and courage. It also helps in legal matters, cleansing negative attitudes, achieving your goals, and bringing enthusiasm and happiness. You can also use orange to attract friends, and inspire emotional healing.

-Pink – The color pink is representative of all variations of love, including romantic, friendly, universal, and spiritual. Use pink for forgiveness, compassion, harmony, joy, sensitivity, spiritual and emotional healing, self-love, and for making love spells.

-Red – The color of passion and fire, red represents action and activity, love, blood, fertility, sex, power, potency, courage, and vitality. It imparts strength and energy. Thus, you can use it for vigor, defense, and health. It is also a symbol of the Triple Goddess' Mother aspect. You can use it to represent or invoke the Fire element.

-Purple – A highly spiritual color, purple is connected to spiritual awakening, psychic abilities, and ancient wisdom. It's the color of the 3rd eye chakra where your inner eye and psychic vision reside. Thus, you can use it to help open your 3rd eye. This will allow you to enhance your intuition and invite visions. You can also use purple for healing, spiritual protection, honor, respect, purification, wisdom, progress, sensitivity, dissociating from your ego, and spiritual growth. Meditate with a purple candle on a regular basis to relieve insomnia or lower stress levels.

-Magenta – Magenta facilitates fast results in spells, as well as quick changes. Burn it with another candle of a different color to raise the energy level of a candle's intent and purpose. You can also use magenta for spiritual healing and exorcism.

-Blue – A soothing color, blue is associated with inner peace, harmony, and spirituality. It promotes tranquility, truth, wisdom, healing, rest, patience, kindness, and serenity. Burn it for prophetic dreams and some dream magick. It encourages understanding, a peaceful home, and loyalty. A blue candle can represent or invoke the water element. To focus your mind, you can meditate with a blue-colored candle.

-Turquoise – Use turquoise for intellect and focus, and to relieve stress. It helps in improving memory, storing knowledge, and finding logic and reason in any given situation.

-Green – Green represents growth, fertility, and nature. It is the symbol of the Green Earth goddess. Green is also the color of financial success and money. You can use it for prosperity and luck, generosity and abundance, emotional and physical healing, earth magick, renewal, and rejuvenation. In agriculture, green helps encourage a good harvest. You can use green to represent the Earth element.

-Brown – The color of earth, brown holds a balanced, grounded vibration. It promotes decision-making and clear thinking. It is also good for intuition, material gain, concentration, common sense, wealth, and stability. Brown stimulates intuition as well as telepathic abilities. You can use it to find missing objects. You can also use brown to heal and protect animals.

-Silver (or Gray) – This is a neutral color. You can use it to neutralize and deflect negative energy. It provides protection from otherworldly entities, promotes serenity and inner peace, and stabilizes energies. It is a symbol of the fertility goddess.

-Gold – Gold is associated with solar deities and the supreme god. It helps attract cosmic powers and influences. Gold also promotes communication, wealth, success, masculine energy, persuasion, confidence, and victory. Use it to invoke any of the male deities.

-Black – Black absorbs all colors. It is often used to banish or absorb negativity. It helps reverse hexes and curses. Use black to repel and banish black magick, for protection and to get rid of bad habits. It promotes self-control and resilience, and inner strength. You can also use it for meditation. This will help you dive deeper into the unconscious. Burn black for potent healing and support for grief and loss. Black represents the Triple Goddess' Crone aspect.

How to Choose Your Candles

When looking for one-spell candles, chime candles are ideal to use because of their diminutive size. For longer rituals that may take a few days to perform, you can use votive or taper candles.

Pillar and jar candles last the longest. Often used for folk magick, these candles help magical intent and prayers direct to the spirit world. To add more life to your spells, you can opt for ritually-charged candles. These were created and charged with particular magickal intent, and you don't even need to cast a spell. You can just light the candle as you state your intent.

A spell candle is potent only when it is burning, whether or not you are using it in a formal spell. You can find a wide array of available candles – from love spell to protection candles.

Candle Spells for Money, Luck, and Wealth

Financial Flame

This is an easy spell to attract money and wealth into your life. You won't find a lot of money spells around.

What you'll need:

- 2 candles; one green and one gold

- Pine incense

- Patchouli incense

- A few pieces of acorn

- A piece of paper

How to do it:

At the bottom part of each candle, carve out a Fehu rune. Arrange the candles one across one another in holders. Place the patchouli incense beside the gold candle, then the pine next to the green candle. Light everything up to get the incense burning.

On the sheet of paper, draw another Fehu. Put the acorns at the top. If acorns aren't available, you can use smooth stones instead. Both acorns and smooth stones represent Earth energy and wealth in spells.

Allow the candles to burn down completely. Leave the acorns on the altar. Don't take them away until extra money begins to flow your way.

Shimmering Silver Spell

This prosperity spell will help bring you some extra money. However, it's important not to be too greedy, or the spell won't work. Like other prosperity spells or magick involving money, this spell is associated with the Earth element. It is best that you perform the spell on a full moon. The night must be clear so the moonlight will come in through the window.

What you'll need:

- 7 fresh basil leaves

- 1 cauldron

- Water (spring or rain)

- 1 silver coin

How to do it:

If you can't find a cauldron, you can use a ceramic bowl, instead. But, never use a metal bowl for the spell. Also, make sure that the coin has silver content. An old dime would be great for this spell.

Place the coin at the cauldron's bottom. Pour some water over it. Make sure that the cauldron is at least half full. Put it on a table or in a window. Let the moonlight shine on it.

Drop the basil leaves, one at a time, into the water. As you do this, say:

By the moonlight

Bless me soon

Silver and water shine

Let wealth be mine.

Leave the cauldron overnight. The following morning throw the basil and water in the backyard. Take the coin, and place it in your pocket.

Home Blessing Candle Spell

Through your candles' bright warmth, you can attract happiness and luck into your home.

What you'll need:

- 3 purple or blue candles

- 1 sandalwood incense stick

- 1 frankincense incense stick

- 1 rosemary incense stick

- 1 bell

- 3 copper pennies

How to do it:

Make sure your candles are large enough to fit a penny in the candle holder underneath. Set up the candles in an even triangle. Then, put a penny each in the candle holder underneath.

Light up one of the candles, then say:

Bring me hope

Light up the sandalwood incense. Ring the bell.

Light up the second candle, then say

Bring me peace.

Light up the frankincense incense. Ring the bell.

Light up the third candle, then say the words

Bring me good fortune.

Light up the rosemary incense. Ring the bell for the last time.

Arrange the incense burners inside the candle triangle. Allow everything to burn for no less than one hour. It is best to do it during the afternoon, but it is not necessary. Afternoons are ideal for getting the incense energy flowing through your home. Snuff the candles out when you're done.

Abundance Spell

Use this spell if you are facing financial difficulties. The flame's energy will help attract new financial opportunities for you.

What you'll need:

- 1 green candle

- Vanilla oil or extract

- Cinnamon oil

- 1 large denomination coin

How to do it:

Get a sharp object and carve out the word "wealth" on the side of the green candle. Anoint the word using vanilla and cinnamon oil. Place the coin at the bottom of the candle holder. Put the candle on top of the coin. Light up the candle, and allow it to completely burn out.

Once the candle is melted, store the wax-covered large denomination coin in a safe place. This will attract money into your life.

Flames of Progress

There is a specific idea behind this spell. Do it to help you move on from any issue that may be stuck. This could be about relationships, money, or anything else. You can use this spell if you've been waiting for something, maybe a response, that never comes, or if you lack the motivation to move on. Whatever your actual purpose may be, this spell can help you gain some progress.

What you'll need:

•   1 white candle

•   1 dark blue candle

•   1 pale blue candle

•   Something sharp you can use to inscribe runes on the candles

•   Cinnamon incense

How to do it:

Carve the rune thurisaz at the center of the white candle. Carve raidho on the light blue candle, and jera on the blue candle. Place the candles in ah holder. The white candle should be on your left, the dark blue candle on your right, and the pale blue candle at the center.

While holding the cinnamon incense with your left hand, focus on the issue you want to work on. Light up the incense, making sure not to blow it at once. Use its flame to light up the white candle. Blow the incense out, and set it on a holder.

Speak these words aloud:

With this flame, I light the spell.

I need to move on, and not to sit.

Use the flame from the lit candle to light up the second candle, then say:

With this flame, the spell will go on.

As of now, there is no more delay.

Now, light up the last candle with the middle candle. Complete the words of your spell:

With this flame, I now cast the spell.

Things will begin to move at last.

Look at each of the candles. Repeat the words of the spell in the exact same order. Allow them to burn on the altar until they burn out on their own. You'll begin to notice some changes or progress within a short period of time.

Candle Spells for Relieving Tension and Negativity

Burning the Negativity Away

If you feel any negative energy or unnecessary tension in your life, this Wiccan candle spell can help. You don't need to have bad energy at home to use this spell. When anything is getting you down, feel free to perform this ritual.

What you'll need:

- 1 black candle

- Dried basil, mint and/or white sage

- Sandalwood oil

How to do it:

Crush the dried herbs into very small pieces. Bigger pieces will not be effective in your spell. Rub sandalwood oil all over the black candle until it is slick and nice. Roll the candle on the herbs to allow them to stick well over the candle's surface.

Place the candle on a holder, then light it up. There may be some sparks when the herbs and oil begin to burn. This, you should pick a safe location for the spell. As the candle is burning, say the following phrases:

I banish all negative energies,

I banish all poor spirits,

I banish all bad attitudes,

I welcome peace and happiness.

Repeat the phrases three times. Allow the candle to burn down totally. If any wax remains, bury it in your backyard.

The Light of Joy

The spell is for your household. It will help reduce tensions that are turning into problems. It will bring in joy and happiness for your entire family. It will also work with roommates.

What you'll need:

- 1 pink candle

- 4 candles of different colors (with no 2 candles of the same color)

- 1 handful of fresh basil

- Sandalwood incense

- Large-sized piece of clear quartz

How to do it:

You can perform the spell on an altar, if you have one. But, a better idea is to set it up in a central area of your home.

Form a circle with the 5 candles. Place the crystal at the center. Then, lay the basil leaves on top. Light up the candles.

Light up the candles, and then the incense. Carry it through all your home's main rooms. Do it slowly to allow the smoke to spread out. Once done, take the incense back to where the candles are.

Allow everything to burn out on their own. Soon, you will find all the conflict and tension in your home gone.

Don't expect the spell to fix everything. There may be specific active problems your household may currently be experiencing. You need to work them out first.

Spell for arguments

You can use this spell for times when resentment is lingering in the air, and it is preventing you from making amends with your friend. The spell can help brighten up the day and rejuvenate your friendship.

What you'll need:

- 1 bay leaf (it's ok even if dry)

- 1 small-sized paper envelope

- 1 yellow candle

How to do it:

On one of the envelope's sides, write your name, then write the name of your friend on the other side. Insert the bay leaf inside the envelope, then seal the envelope. Light up the candle. Hold up the envelope towards the flame until it begins to burn. It is a good idea to have a heat-proof bowl on hand where you can place the paper as it burns. This way, you can prevent hurting your fingers.

Simple Space Cleansing

This candle spell will help keep all negative energy away from your space. It is ideal for use for a single room, instead of the entire home.

What you'll need:

- 1 blue taper candle

- Salt

- A square of white paper

How to do it:

Lay down the paper on the table or altar. Set up the candle at the center. If there is one available, use a candleholder made of clear glass. Otherwise, any kind will do. Drizzle a circle of salt on the paper, making sure that all the four corners of the piece of paper touch the salt.

Light up the candle once the clock strikes the top of the hour. This means at exactly 1:00 AM, 2:00 AM, 5 PM, etc. Let the candle burn on its own, then bury the piece of paper outside your home. Once done, all the negative energy in the room will be gone.

New Beginning Candle Spell

This one is a great multi-purpose spell that you can use to provide a little "oomph" to something new in your life. This can be a new relationship, a new job, or simply a new page in your life. This is very easy to do as well.

What you'll need:

• 2 white taper candles

• Some rosemary oil

How to do it:

Anoint the 2 candles with oil. Place them in candle holders arranged side by side. Light up one candle. Speak about some things you want to remove in your life. Concentrate on them for several minutes. Use the lit candle to light up the other candle, then snuff the first candle out.

Now, write down some new things you hope to attract into your life for this new beginning. Be realistic, but be optimistic as well. Let the second candle burn out until it is completely done. You may keep the first candle and use it for another spell, if you wish.

Happiness Candle Spell

Do you need to infuse some joy into your life? If yes, then this easy spell can help you view things in a more positive light.

What you'll need:

- 2 orange candles

- Dried lavender

How to do it:

Place several pinches of dried lavender on the table or alter between the candles. Light up both of them, then allow your hands to feel the warmth coming from the flames. Say the following 7 times:

Please bless this spell

For my own happiness

Allow the candles to burn down on their own. In no time, you will find joy in your heart again.

Candle Dream Spells

The Light of Three

This psychic dream spell will deliver dreams that will provide the answers to questions that may be lingering in your mind.

What you'll need:

- 1 3-wick candle inside a jar

- 1 piece of amethyst

- Sandalwood oil

- Dried mugwort

How to do it:

Many home décor stores offer 3-wick candles, although these candles are not as common as the typical candles you see. If you cannot find one for this spell, you can just use a simple white candle.

Think about the question that you want the answers to, while working on the spell. Sprinkle some mugwort all over the candle's surface. Anoint the amethyst using a bit of sandalwood oil.

Let the oiled stone touch your forehead 3x in a triangle. Request the universe to open your third eye. Place the stone at the top of the candle, right in the middle of the wicks. Hold up both your hands over the candle. Say your question out loud. Light up the wicks, then ask the question again.

Once you're done, take note of everything that happens in your dreams for the next three days. You will notice a recurring symbol or pattern. That will be your answer.

Dream Seeing Spell

You can awaken the inner psychic in you using a candle. The spell will attract intuitive dreams as you sleep.

What you'll need:

•	1 white candle

•	1 small-sized square of silver and/or purple fabric

•	1 large-sized piece of amethyst

•	1 black marker

How to do it:

Using the marker, draw the image of an eye on the fabric, candle, and stone. Place everything on the altar. Light up the candle.

Put the stone on the silver/purple fabric in a way that the eyes touch. Visualize that you have an eye on your forehead that you can open to look into your dreams.

Touch it to your forehead. Make sure the image of the eye is rubbing against your skin.

As you watch the candle, utter the words:

Open sight.

Say the phrase repeatedly as you focus on the flame.

Set the fabric back on the table. Allow the candle to fully burn out. Once done, take the fabric. Place it underneath your pillow as you sleep. This will bring you psychic dreams.

Candle Love Spells

Red Triad Love Spell

In Wicca, the number 3 is quite powerful. This is why a lot of spells use it. This love spell is no exception.

What you'll need:

- 3 thin candles (the taper type)

- A length of red string or yarn

- Rose oil

- Lavender oil

- Yarrow oil

- Something sharp you can use to inscribe on the candles

How to do it:

Carve out a heart with a small pentacle inside each of the candles. You don't have to make it perfect. Even a rough symbol would be fine. Anoint every candle with the oils (one candle, one type of oil). Bind them together using the yarn. This way, their symbols all touch the group's middle. Tie the string or yarn into a bow. Set it up in a dish or candle holder. As you light up the candles, say the following words:

Live, life, love

I ask this from above.

Three multiplied by three

Bring them all to me.

Allow the candles to burn down about 1/3 of the way, then put the flame out. Repeat the steps for the following two nights until the candles completely burn out. Soon, you'll find a sign about someone entering your life for a new romance.

Mend the Rift in a Relationship

Use this spell if you are experiencing problems in your relationship. This may include a big fight or any type of division. The spell can help you make things better. It will not mend fundamental differences between you and your partner. But, the spell can help both of you get over difficult things that may have happened.

What you'll need:

- 1 white candle

- 1 thin lavender candle

- Some powdered dry basil

How to do it:

Make sure to have some patience as this spell can be a bit tricky to put together. Crack the lavender candle in half without cutting the wick. This way, the wax is broken, but you can still see the wick running intact through both pieces.

As you work on the spell, concentrate on the rift you're attempting to mend. Think of how you can make things better if you had one more chance.

Rub basil on the broken, rough ends of the pieces of candle. Make them fit together as close as possible. Light up the white candle, then drip some wax over the broken part. Do this until the lavender candle is mended back into a single piece.

Set the lavender candle on a holder, then light it up. Allow it to burn until the flame reaches the area of the break. Sit while holding the candle. Concentrate on the flame while it passes through the point where the pieces are joined. Think about how you can improve your relationship.

Once the flame has passed the split, allow the rest of the candle to burn out in a normal manner. Observe how your relationship improves within the next few days.

Candle Melding Love Spell

You can bring that lost or waning romance back with this spell. Use it when you and your partner are apart because of circumstances like work and school. You can also use it if you just broke up. As the candle wax melds together slowly, you will slowly get back together again.

What you'll need:

- 2 red candles in human figure (regular red candles will do if human figure candles aren't available)

- Ginger oil

How to do it:

Anoint the candles with some oil. Put them in a dish or candle holder side by side. Using separate candle holders may be ineffective because the candles need to touch one another.

Light the 2 candles. Then, as the wax starts to run and mix between the candles, focus on your loved one. Concentrate on the spell until the 2 candles are joined together by melted wax.

Say the words

Candles burn; wax will run

You and I are one again.

Repeat the chant a few times or until you feel that you have made your point. Allow the candles to burn out on their own. Do not snuff them out.

Birds of the Same Feather Spell

The goal of this spell is to help you in finding someone who is similar to you in many ways. This someone shares some of your personality traits and interests. This really depends on your preference. They say that opposites attract. If this does not apply to you and you want to find someone like you, don't worry, as this spell can also help.

Before you perform the spell, it is worth mentioning that the smell of burning feather is quite unpleasant. Thus, you should do it outside or at least, near an open window.

What you'll need:

- 1 large natural feather

- Rose oil

- 1 pink candle

- 1 cup of water

- Lavender incense

How to do it:

Anoint the candle, then light up the incense. Focus on the qualities you want your partner to have. Wave the feather through the incense smoke. Light the feather tip in the candle frame. Then, point it to the west direction. As you do this, repeat the spell words several times:

Bring to me my match

Bring to me my mate

With this feather,

I won't wait

Now, hold the feather (better if still smoldering) close to your heart. Then utter the words:

Air and smoke

I dare, by magick

Birds of the same feather

Flock together

Drop the last piece of feather in the water. Sprinkle a drop of rose oil. Leave the cup on the altar. Soon, you will come across someone similar to you, one way or another.

Come Back to Me Candle Spell

You find love, but you lose it. It's a sad story, but it happens. Don't worry. Here's another spell to bring back a loved one who has gone away. This is quite a popular and easy spell.

What you'll need:

- 1 pink, white, or red candle

- Red string or yarn

- Vanilla oil

How to do it:

Get something sharp you can use to inscribe your own initials with on the candle (around halfway down). Then, inscribe your beloved's initials over yours. Note that you should write over the letters of your initials, and not ON TOP.

Anoint the candle with some vanilla oil. Tie the string or yarn around the candle using a bow. Make sure the knot is lying over the carved initials. Light up the candle, and allow it to burn until it gets to the point where the initials are.

Blow out the candle gently. Place it on the altar with the goal of finishing it once your loved one comes back. Until then, add some oil to the initials every day.

Return of a Lover Incense

Although this is not a complete spell, you can burn this incense blend to help your lost loved one find their way back to you. After all, no one says that spells need to be complicated.

What you'll need:

- Ground cardamom

- Charcoal

- Dragon's blood resin

How to do it:

This is easy to do, but you may need to drop by the nearest occult shop to buy some dragon's blood resin.

All you have to do to perform the spell is to blend the resin and cardamom together. Sprinkle the mixture on a lit up charcoal tablet. Allow the smoke to drift out of the window. This will help draw your lost lover back to you.

Midsummer Rose Candle Spell

This is a popular spell to get back with an ex-lover. You must be very determined to make it happen though, because this spell will only work one day in a year – midsummer's eve or June 20. Make sure that date is not far away when you need to use the spell.

It is actually an easy spell to perform, but it requires a bit of legwork. This is particularly true if you reside in a big city. In case you don't know yet, the longest day in a year happens on Midsummer. This often falls on June 20 or 21. Midsummer Eve is the evening of the 19th or 20th.

What you'll need:

- 5 red roses

- A church

- A crossroads

- Tree with a bird's nest

- Natural running water such as a stream

How to do it:

You need to pick out the locations ahead of time. But, you have to make sure that you can do everything by Midsummer's Eve.

Bury one rose under your tree. Set another rose near the church gate, one rose near the running water, and another at the point where two roads cross. Place the 5th rose under your pillow. Sleep using the pillow with the rose for three nights.

On night 4, pluck the rose's petals. Leave a few petals at the other 4 locations where you set the other roses. Before you know it, your ex will be running right back to your waiting arms.

Found Coin Spell

Being left behind by a loved one is a common problem that we encounter at least once during our lifetime. This is another spell to bring an ex-lover back that you can try.

What you'll need:

• A length of red yarn

• 1 pinch of rosemary (preferably fresh, but dry will do)

• 1 small paper envelope

• 1 coin you found outside

How to do it:

On the inner side of the envelope, write the name of your ex. Rub some rosemary on the coin. While holding both the coin and rosemary in your hand, say the name of your ex 4 times. Whenever you say it, face one of the directions of the elements (east, west, north, and south.) Don't turn aimlessly. Use a compass if necessary.

Seal the coin inside the envelope, then roll it up into a tube. Kiss it, then keep it rolled by tying the yarn around it. Keep it in a place that is special to you.

Take the used rosemary, and fling it into the breeze. As you do this, make a fervent wish for the person you love to come back to you.

Jumping Bean Spell

This spell is ideal to use to bring you back together with someone who left because of family, school, work, or something similar. To make the spell work, you may need to do some shopping for supplies. This is because some materials are often not available in your household – unless your magickal inventory is well-stocked!

What you'll need:

- 1 human-figure candle

- 1 heat resistant bowl

- Tonka beans

How to do it:

If tonka beans are not available, you can instead use some dry beans if you have them in your pantry. If possible, perform the spell on a full moon, and on a Friday night.

Carve out the name of your loved one along the candle's side. Light up the candle as you think about your lover who is away.

Put 3 beans inside the bowl, and set it under a small fire. If you find it inconvenient to make your own fire, just use one of your stove's burners.

As soon as the beans start to snap and jump, utter your loved one's name aloud. Wish that the spell will also make them move back into your life. Put out the candle's flame.

Repeat the spell for two nights more. Have faith that the spell will make your wish come true, and it will.

Be Mine Bath Spell

One refreshing way to win back your ex-lover is to soak in a wonderful rose-scented bath. Here's a spell that will make you smell as sweet as a flower as you await the return of your loved one.

What you'll need:

- A picture of you with your ex

- 1 cup of pink rose petals

- ½ cup of calendula blossoms

- 2 drops of rose attar

- 2 drops of chamomile essential oil

- A few pieces of pink or white candles

How to do it:

Pick a good photo of you and your loved one together. Choose one that was taken during your happy days together. Make sure to cut out images of other people, leaving only the two of you.

If you don't have a picture together, you can use separate photos. Just cut them up, then tape your images together. Now, if you don't have any pictures at all, then consider other spells, instead. You cannot use this spell.

Prepare a warm bath. Light up the candles. The candles are intended more to set up the right atmosphere. How many candles you set up doesn't really matter.

Scatter the petals and essential oil to the water. You may first wrap the flowers in cheesecloth loosely if you don't feel like the idea of picking up wet flowers later.

Tape or pin the picture on the wall in such a way that you can see it clearly as you soak in the tub. Enjoy your bath for as long as possible, all the while focusing on the photo. Think about the happier times with your ex-lover. Concentrate on bringing back the happy times in your life.

Put the photo on the altar after your bath. Wait for your loved one to come back. You won't have to wait for a long time!

Perfect Partner Spell

Candles set the perfect tone for a romantic dinner. But, for this spell? Well, you don't actually use a candle for the early part of the spell. At the right time, however, you will see some flickers.

While you can use the spell to draw a particular person into your life, the best results happen when you allow the universe to deliver the right person for you. Thus, when performing the spell, refrain from using any name or focusing on a specific person.

What you'll need:

• 1 white candle

- 1 candle of your preferred color (not white)

- 2 candle holders (1 for each candle)

- Pink chalk

- Pink or red cloth

How to do it:

Find a clear space in your home to set up the altar, in case you don't have one yet. Note that it will take a few days for the spell to work.

With 1 hand, hold the white candle and concentrate on the traits you want to find in a partner. Enumerate them out loud while you focus on the candle, which represents your future partner.

Pick up the other candle. Say all the traits you'll bring into the new relationship. The second candle represents you.

Lay the pink cloth out. Place the candles with their holders on opposite sides of the cloth (around 2' apart). At the center, between the 2 candles, use the chalk to draw a large heart.

Every night, focus on the candles and think about the ideal relationship you're searching for. Then, move the 2 candles closer together. Move them a bit closer each night until the candles meet at the center of your drawn heart.

Now, you may be wondering how many days it will take before the two candles meet. It depends on how far you space the candles. Just make sure it is not less than one week.

Once the candles are next to each other inside the heart, draw a second heart surrounding the first heart.

Ask the goddess Aphrodite (or another love goddess you prefer) to grant your wish. Then, light up the candles.

On succeeding nights, light up the candles and allow them to burn for as long as possible until they burn out. Have patience because the spell might not work right away. It may take some time.

Key to Your Heart Candle Spell

This spell requires little time to do, but the charm will take around 2 weeks to complete. Don't worry because the results will make the wait worthwhile. You will find a new love after you have cast the spell.

What you'll need:

- 1 gold candle

- 1 silver candle

- 1 red candle

- 2 red roses

- 1 key

- 1 horseshoe

- 1 red silk scarf

How to do it:

Like most other love spells, this is best performed on a Friday night.

First, light up the candles. Then, use the silk scarf to wrap the roses, key, and horseshoe together. Pass the scarf with the items through the candle flames' heat, making sure that it does not catch fire. Place it in the drawer where you put your underwear. Leave it there for two weeks.

After two weeks, bury the roses in your backyard. Keep the key and horseshoe safely near your bed. Within a month, expect to welcome a new person to love in your life.

Kiss of Aphrodite

Harness Aphrodite's mighty power through this love spell. The goddess will help attract true love to you.

What you'll need:

- 5 pink candles

- 5 red candles

- 5 white candles

- Deep red lipstick

- 1 clean sea shell

- 1 square piece of white cloth

- 1 small-sized white dish

- 1 piece of red ribbon or yarn

- Fresh strawberries

How to do it:

Prepare the altar first. Make sure that there will be no distractions once you start the spell and while it is active.

Create three candle rings, with the white candles inside the ring, and the red and pink candles outside. The size of the rings depends on your preference. Light up all the 15 candles. Light one ring of candles at a time, beginning with the white candles.

Here's the initial part of the spell that you must say out loud:

By the mighty Aphrodite's power

I request the goddess to bless this ritual

To bring forth to me a true love

So let it be done.

Put on some lipstick. It's ok to do this even if you're not a woman, just for performing this spell. Place a big lip print at the center of the white cloth. Then, say the following out loud:

With this shell,

I call on the Goddess

To bring forth to me a true love

So let it be done.

Run your hands through each of the candle circles, just a little above the flames. Start again with the white candles inside, then move outwards. Place the dish inside the circle. Place a berry or two on the dish. The berries represent the goddess Aphrodite.

Let all the candles naturally burn out on their own. It's not important which candle colors go out first. Keep everything in place, and don't move anything until your wish has been granted. If no new relationship enters your life. Wait for at least a full moon cycle before trying the ritual again.

A Call to the Universe

The simple spell will allow you to ask the Universe for help in bringing your lost lover back. This is ideal for use when you have tried everything else, but failed. The results may take some time to manifest, but have faith and they will happen.

What you'll need:

- 1 pink candle

- 1 flower (preferably a rose, but any other flower will do)

- 1 stick of sandalwood incense

- 1 stick of rose incense

- 1 stick of frankincense incense

How to do it:

Perform the spell under the moonlight outdoors, preferable during the waxing moon phase.

Set up the flower in a vase, then light up the candle, followed by the 3 incense sticks.

Watch the smoke of the incense flow through the candle light. Watch it rise up to the sky.

Imagine your wishes traveling with the smoke through the sky, trying to find the person you want to see. Let the incense burn out. Do not lose hope because the person you love will be found.

Joining Together Photo Spell

If your goal is to have somebody stuck on you, this is one of the best love spells to use. You should only use a photo where there's nobody else but you and your target in it.

What you'll need:

- 1 picture of you

- 1 picture of the person you want to be with

- 1 red candle

- 1 pen or marker

How to do it:

At the back of the picture of your target, write the words "I love you." Then, at the back of your own picture, write the words "You love me." Light up the candle as you look at the photos. Imagine you and the other person together for real.

Allow some candle wax to drip on the pictures' front sides. Stick them together as fast as you can, and before the wax dries up. Say the following words:

Together united as one

Under the sun and moon.

Place the photos under your pillow. Keep them there as you sleep. Do this until your loved one comes to you.

Candle Spells for Health, Wellbeing, and Personal Favors

Simple Health Blessing

Bear in mind that the items you use for this spell are meant to represent vitality and health. They do not serve as medical remedies for any ailments. This is an easy spell that you can use to give blessings.

What you'll need:

- 1 glass of apple juice

- 1 white candle

- 1 cinnamon stick

How to do it:

In putting out spells, it is often a great idea to use natural ingredients. Thus, for this health blessing spell, try to find organic apple juice, when possible.

Pour the apple juice in a glass. Stir 4 times using the cinnamon stick. Light up the white candle. Take a few sips of the juice.

Repeat the following phrases:

Goddess bless the body and soul

Health and wellness are my goals

Finish off the rest of the apple juice, then snuff the candle out. Perform the spell each time you feel the onset of an ailment. You can also do it every morning jut to keep yourself in top shape.

Confidence Candle Spell

Improving your trust and confidence in yourself goes a long way in helping you cope in all aspects of your life. Through this candle spell, you will love yourself even more.

What you'll need:

- Pink and white rose petals

- 1 pink candle

- Pure water

How to do it:

For best results, use natural water. But, if you do not like consuming your local rain water, you can just buy some spring water. Although it is not ideal for use in this spell, you can use tap water as well if you don't have other options.

Arrange the flower petals into a ring on the table or altar. Set up the pink candle at the center. Do not light it up yet. First, think about your best traits, and focus on them for several minutes. Then, light up the candle. Repeat the following words several times:

Let my own light shine bright

With divine love.

Take a long sip of water. This will help get rid of all your negative thoughts. Allow the candle to completely burn out on its own.

Truth Candle Spell

This spell can help you find the truth in any given situation. If you feel there is something being hidden from you on purpose, or you are confused about a particular situation in your life, this spell can help.

What you'll need:

•   1 lapis lazuli gemstone (make sure to cleanse first before using) or lapis lazuli orgonite

•   1 white or purple candle

How to do it:

Ground and center yourself, then cast a circle. Light up the candle, and focus on the flame's light for several minutes. As you do this, clear your mind of all thoughts.

Hold the crystal in your hand. Close your eyes, and try to see the bright white flame using your mind's eye.

Witness the flame as it grows bigger and bigger, until it fills the entire circle with light.

Strengthen the light as much as you can. Try to hold the image for a few minutes. Then, send off the light into the crystal in your hand. Visualize how the lapis lazuli stone absorbs all the light in the circle. Watch it glow brighter than even 1000 flames.

Say the following aloud:

May the truth I am seeking

To me be revealed

May what is hidden

Be brought to light

So let it be done.

Now, close the circle. The crystal has been enchanted to show the truth in the given situation. Before going to sleep, put the crystal underneath your pillow. Think that the truth will be revealed to you through your dreams. Note that it isn't necessary for you to recall your dreams for the spell to work. It will manifest in the form of gut feelings and intuition during the day.

Keep the crystal wrapped in white cloth whenever you do not need it. Don't allow anyone, except yourself, to handle it.

Chapter 3: Crystal Spells

Crystals are not only ornamental and nice to look at. Wiccans perform some of their most potent spells with the help of gemstones and crystals. They carry various crystals with them on a regular basis – for protection, and to attract different energies.

For a beginner, delving into the world of crystals can be a bit overwhelming. The sheer volume of available crystals can make your head pop! But, you don't have to worry. In this chapter, we'll not only discuss the different crystals that are often used in Wiccan spells. We will also cover which crystals are ideal for use for specific spells, and how to use them.

Using Crystals

Wiccans use crystals to perform spells because of the stones' ability to harness magickal energy. When using a crystal, you focus your intent, energy, and power into the crystal. You combine them with the incredible magickal properties that are already in the crystal. This will make your spells and rituals more powerful.

When working with crystals, you must first cleanse them to get rid of the residual energy that they may still hold. There are several ways to do this:

- Running water – Cleanse the crystal using running water.

- Full moon – Allow the crystal to sit under the full moon.

- Burying – You can bury the crystal on the earth.

- Sage – You can use sage to cleanse your crystals.

If you some research, you'll find a lot of different crystal cleansing methods you can choose from. Just like performing magick, choosing a method for cleansing is personal. Stick with whatever works for you, and whatever you find convenient. What is important is to make sure that whatever method you choose, it will not cause damage to your crystal!

Once you have decided to use crystals for your spell work, you must learn the different ways to use the stones. These include:

•   Sleeping with the crystal – Put the crystal under your pillow, and sleep with it.

•   Holding the crystal – If you are comfortable doing it, then go ahead.

•   Keeping the crystal nearby. – Place the crystal on your night table or somewhere near your bed.

Having crystals like selenite, jasper, and amethyst near you while you sleep can promote relaxation and rest. There are crystals that can help you remember your dreams – and interpret them!

Carrying a crystal with you all the time can promote concentration, honesty, and communication. If this is inconvenient with you, especially if you have a regular day job, you can just slip it inside your purse. This way, you will always be within the scope of your crystal's protective properties.

Write down your spells or make a list of intentions, then place the crystal on top like a paperweight. This will help incorporate the crystals into your physical spell work.

For best results, write a list of your intentions, then find a crystal that can help you achieve them. Place the crystal on top of the list to allow the stone to supercharge your intentions list. Leave it on your altar or a shelf so it will remain undisturbed. Just visit it anytime you feel necessary.

Crystals can be used as energy cleansers as well. There are different types of crystals that have the capability to get rid of negative energy. For example, you can use a crystal while taking a shower to clean out all negative feelings that you may be harboring.

You can also use crystals to direct energy – just like a magic wand! If you are working with a crystal point, use the point to lead the energy of the crystal to go wherever you like.

While holding the crystal, you may feel a vibration or tremble. This is good because it means you and the crystal are in tune, and you are able to harness its powers!

Most Common Crystals Used in Wiccan Spells

As mentioned, there is a wide variety of crystals to use for your spells. This makes choosing which particular stone to use for a particular spell difficult. Because of this, a lot of beginners quickly get distracted and overwhelmed. Don't be.

In this section, we'll discuss the most common crystals used for casting spells. While the list may not complete, it is enough to help you get on your way to mastering the use of crystals.

-Agate – The crystal will help you, the spell caster, restore your energy and healing power. A grounding stone, agate promotes intellect and creativity. Because of its high protective qualities, it is often used for protection spells for children.

-Amber – Depending on your intent, amber can provide the calming energy in your spells. At the same time, it will help energize you as the caster. Amber is also a good luck charm. It helps draw out all negativity, and help relieve physical pain. It is known to bring positive energy to the user or wearer.

-Amethyst – Ancient Greeks wore the purple stone to relieve the effects of too much drinking. Since then, amethyst has become known for its calming properties, and its ability to treat various ailments. The stone also helps control harmful behavior. It is also used often in scrying work because it promotes psychic awareness.

-Citrine – Many Wiccans never leave home without this crystal. This is because citrine helps cleanse negative energy. It also provides mental stimulation and enhances focus. It is a great crystal to use for employment-related matters. This is because the crystal also promotes communication and honesty.

-Emerald – The birthstone for May, emerald comes in various shades of green. But, regardless of greenness, any emerald promotes imagination and creativity. The stone is also ideal for use in spells that involve love, domestic matters, prosperity, and fertility.

-Hematite – Hematite can be used as a staple in almost all crystal workings. It provides grounding and protection. It also promotes a balanced mind, body, and spirit.

-Jade – You can use jade whenever you need help with your dreams, interpreting your dreams, to be more specific. It also enhances self-sufficiency and confidence.

-Jasper – The stone for travelers, jasper comes in 3 colors: red, yellow, and brown. Red jasper provides protection. Yellow jasper helps clear your mind. Brown is ideal to use for grounding and concentration purposes.

-Moonstone – The crystal is known for its ability to make the owner's feminine aspects emerge. It also enhances one's confidence, and brings about calmness and awareness.

-Obsidian – This is another stone that is ideal for grounding. With its jet black color, obsidian comes with protection, clarity, and healing properties.

-Onyx – Onyx is a black stone. It is used to get rid of negativity. It also promotes good decision-making, and helps attract fortune and happiness.

Quartz – You may find quartz in many various forms. But, regardless of the form, quartz is great to have on hand. It will help clear your mind, and amplify the properties of other crystals nearby. Clear quartz is often used for healing, logic, and creating a safe area for medication. The rose quartz variety is ideal for children. It is called the "mother stone." It provides protection, opens up your imagination, and enhances happiness and love. Blue quartz is a great aid for concentration, and this makes it popular among students.

Working with different crystals can be a lot of fun. You have the freedom to use whichever works bestfor you. To be on the safe side at all times, do your research first. Take things slow. Keep an observant eye, and see which stones feel right for you.

Crystal Spells for Beginners

Like candle spells, you can use crystals for different purposes, although the most popular crystal spells involve love. This includes spells to invite new romance into your life, reconcile with a loved one whom you have broken up with, or to bring back someone you love who has gone away.

Some spells aim to affect a specific person. You may also cast generic spells that do not target someone in particular. Whatever purpose you may have for casting a spell, there is a spell that will suit your particular purpose.

But, anything you do will have an effect on you as well. Remember the 2 major rules of Wicca? We are all one with the universe, and the gods and goddesses. So, be careful when putting out a spell.

Having said that, following are some popular examples of love spells that harness the power of crystals:

Reuniting Reflections Spell

Using the mirror's power, this crystal spell aims to reunite you with the person you love. Have faith, and it will happen. But, bear in mind that this spell will only work if you use it on someone who already loves you or who was in love with you before. It will not be successful on someone who has never loved you before.

There are other spells you can use to help you make a specific person love you. But for now, let us focus on bringing a lost loved one back.

What you'll need:

•   1 mirror (make up mirror or one with a stand that you can tilt)

•   1 pen (preferably of high quality ink)

•   1 piece of paper (preferably fine linen paper)

•   A few pieces of rose quartz, red jasper, carnelian, and/or garnet

How to do it:

On the piece of paper, write your full name, then your missing lover's name under it. Arrange the mirror and paper in a way that they are face to face.

Tip the mirror a bit downwards. Make it face the paper without propping up the later.

Put the crystals over your names, then say the following words:

Mirror, mirror can you see?

Bring back to me my lover.

In a few days, expect to hear some news about your loved one. You should be back together again in no time.

Bring Back Bundle Spell

This is a "charm bag" type of spell that will help make your lost loved one come back to you. After making the charm, you must always keep it in your backpack or purse. If this will not be convenient for you, then you might consider trying a different spell instead.

What you'll need:

- Red fabric (around 6" square piece)

- 3 stones you picked up outdoors

- A few saffron threads (you may find this a bit expensive)

- 1 copper coin

- 1 piece of rose quartz

- 3 rose petals

- A length of black heavy yarn

How to do it:

Gather all the materials (except for the yarn). Place everything at the center of the red fabric. Say these words a few times:

May this charm bring (say the name of your ex-lover) back to me.

Magick things, black and red

Bound together, and carried near

Bring back to me what's dear.

Bundle all the items in the fabric. Close it tightly using the black yarn. Carry the charm with you all day. You may leave it near your bed when you sleep. In time, your ex will come back to you.

Bear in mind that this spell will help reunite you with your ex who has gone away. But, it will not help you bring someone new into your life. There are many other spells you can use for that purpose.

The Love Compass

There are times when circumstances force you to lose contact with a loved one. It may be a lover, a friend, or a family member. You can use this spell to help them find their way back to you.

What you'll need:

- 1 compass (a true compass equipped with a movable magnetic needle; your smartphone's GPS device won't do)

- Fresh rose petals

- Dried rosemary

- 1 piece of lodestone or hematite

How to do it:

Place the compass on the altar or table. Make sure you can clearly see the directions. Perform the spell while you are facing towards the west direction. Leave your compass on the altar. The, say the following words:

East, west, north, south

Find the one I love best for me

Where they have gone, I don't know,

Give me some signs because I need them so.

Drizzle a circle of rose petals and rosemary around the compass. Cover everything using the silk cloth. Place the stone above the compass, then say the words again.

Wait for 3 days to pass. On the 4th day, try to look for signs of where you can find your missing loved one. In case you're wondering what the compass does in the spell, the answer is nothing. It's only symbolic. It will not really point the way.

Moonlight Kiss Crystal Love Charm

This spell combines the respective powers of the moon and quartz crystal to attract some new romance into your life.

What you'll need:

- 1 piece of rose quartz crystal

- 1 small-sized silver bowl

- A handful of red or pink rose petals

How to do it:

Perform the ritual on a new moon night. This means the moon is not visible to the earth on that night.

Kiss the crystal, then place it in the silver bowl. Sprinkle some rose petals over the stone, and place it in a window. Leave it alone for 7 days.

After 7 days, get the crystal. Carry it around with you to help draw some exciting romance to your life. Do not touch the bowl of petals. Leave it in the window and do not remove it until the night of the next new moon.

Star of Love

Perform this spell on a clear night. This is because you need to have a clear view of the stars to make the spell work.

What you'll need

*   1 red candle

*   Jasmine incense

*   A few pieces of pink or red crystals like rose quartz, carnelian or garnet

How to do it:

Place all the materials on an open window where you have a nice view of the clear sky. Light up the candle and incense, then look for the brightest star that glows in the sky.

Put the crystals in your hands. Imagine the light of the star pouring energy into them. Say the following to begin the spell:

Star of love, you burn so bright

Help me in my spell tonight

Make me united with my true love

As I will it, so it will be done.

Say the spell words thrice. Then, lay the stones down on the altar, beside the candle. Allow the candle to burn fully on its own.

Heart of the Matter Spell

This simple spell will sow the attraction seed into the heart of someone whom you like to notice you. Hopefully, the attraction will develop into something more serious, such as a long-lasting relationship.

What you'll need:

- 1 small piece of rose quartz

- 1 pink carnation in full bloom

- 1 small piece of pink paper

- 1 pencil or pen

How to do it:

Put the flower in a vase with water. Make sure to help the flower live as long as you can for the attraction spell to work.

On the piece of pink paper, write the name of your target. Tightly fold the paper. Tuck the rose quarts together with the paper into the flower's middle petals. Then, say the following words:

Put this thought in his/her mind,

Put this thought in his heart,

Put this thought in his life

So that we'll never part.

Concentrate on the person. Feel them slowly getting drawn to you. Leave everything as is until the blossom sags completely. Then, bury the flower in your backyard. Save the stone and paper. Set them on your altar. This will help prolong and continue the spell's effect.

Magnetic Attraction Charm

You can use a magnet's literal attraction power to bring someone new into your life. The spell is ideal to use when you don't have a specific person in mind, but you want to have someone to share your life with.

What you'll need:

- Rose oil

- Vanilla oil

- 1 piece of magnetic lodestone

- A length of red thread

How to do it:

If you do not have lodestone on hand (it is hard to find), you may first check the crystals available in your local occult or New Age shops. You can use an actual lodestone pendant if you have one, but it isn't necessary.

Hold the lodestone in your hands. Rub some vanilla and rose oil into it. Visualize the stone drawing powerful energy into you, and slowly drawing the special person into your life.

Use the thread to tie the stone into a kind of necklace. Have it around your neck. If you prefer, you can just carry it around in your purse or inside your pocket. But, the spell will not be as strong.

Now, go out and spend time mingling with your social groups. This will give the stone the opportunity to draw to you that special person you are looking for.

If this spell doesn't work for you, you can try other similar but stronger spells in this section.

Love in Luna

A lot of crystal love spells work with rose quarts, but there are other crystals you can use to perform some love magick. My personal favorite is moonstone as it helps harness the moon's potent power.

What you'll need:

- 3 pieces of moonstone

- 1 pink taper candle

- 3 pieces of silver cord

- Some moon-infused water

How to do it:

First, you need to prepare some moon-infused water. Wait for the full moon, then place a glass bottle containing some water outdoors to allow it to absorb energy from the moonlight. Leave it for a few days, after which, the water will be ready for use in the spell.

Once you are ready, arrange the silver cords in a triangle. At each point, put a moonstone. Use the moon-infused water to anoint the candle. Do this as you say the following words:

Bringing the light of moon down

Bringing to me love soon

For my cause, light a candle

This spell draws love to me.

Place the candle in the middle of the triangle. Then, light it up. Say the words once more.

Now, pick up the moonstones, one at a time. Each time, hold up the moonstone over the flame. Repeat the words with every moonstone.

Allow the candle to burn out completely. Make sure to have all the 3 moonstones with you at all times – until the time you are ready to welcome someone new into your life, and begin a new romance.

Fire in Stone

If you need a spell to help reignite the waning passion between your partner and you, this is the right spell to use. But, this spell will not succeed if your goal is to meet a new person.

What you'll need:

- 1 piece each of garnet, red jasper, and carnelian crystals

- 1 red candle

- 1 ceramic or glass dish

How to do it:

Pick up one of the stones, then whisper the following words into it:

Love in the fire

Love in the stone

Place the stone in the glass dish.

Do exactly the same to the remaining 2 stones.

Light up the candle. Pick it up and hold it in such an angle that it will burn over the crystals.

Love to me, three crystals.

Keep the candle burning. Allow it to drip wax until all the three stones are covered in a way that they are connected in one wax coating. While the wax is still wet, use something sharp to draw the shape of a heart. Wait for the candle to burn out, but do not touch the wax-coated crystals. Leave them on the altar for no less than one week.

The Root of Feelings Spell

Your spell can't go wrong if you harness the power of the elements well. The element of water brings in mystery, emotions, psychic abilities, and dreams into your rituals and spells. This water spell is a good example. Use this spell if you're confused about a particular life situation you are currently in, and you need to sort your emotions out.

What you'll need:

- 1 living potted plant (make sure the pot has lots of holes at the bottom so water can flow out easily once you water it)

- 4 pieces of clear quartz (the pieces must be about the same size; tiny chips will not work)

- 1 large dish or plate to place under the pot

- 1 sheet of pale blue paper

How to do it:

On the pale blue paper, jot down the different emotions that confuse you. Cut the paper into a circle, then fit the pieces into the plate. It's alright if the paper is much smaller than the plate. What's important is to make sure you cut it into a circle. Set the dish, then put the quartz pieces in a square shape.

Now, this part can be a bit tricky. Place the pot on top of the crystals as balanced as possible. Then, think about every emotion you have over your current situation. Do this as you slowly pour some fresh water on the plant. Make sure to pour enough water to ensure that it flows through the plant's roots, and soak the paper.

While the water is draining through, say the following words:

Water fall, water drain,

Get to the roots of the problem.

Water fall, water drain.

Shatter all my confusion away.

Now, hold one of the plant's leaves with both your hands. Repeat the words of the spell.

For the next 3 days, observe how your emotions start to clear up. Soon, you will experience a solid feeling on where you stand on the matter.

Chapter 4: Herbal Spells

Herbalism is the practice that involves the use of plants for therapeutic or medicinal purposes. It is also called botanical medicine or herbology. There are various ways to use herbs. These include tinctures, teas, and ointments. They are also used for herbal baths.

In Wicca, herbs do not only serve medicinal purposes. They are also used for their magickal properties. This is because herbs hold the energy of the Earth inside them. The energy harnessed from the herbs help make spells more effective.

Different Herb Forms

Herbs are useful, whether dried or fresh, and even in the form of an essential oil. If you want fresh herbs, you can grow them on your own. You can then dry or freeze your excess produce for future use.

Even if you don't have a garden, you can still grow herbs at home. You can use your balcony and even your windowsill. You can even grow different herbs in the same pot, depending of course on the herb type. Good examples are lavender and rosemary.

The best time to harvest your herbs is during the morning, just before the daytime heat sets in. You can resort to drying herbs to prolong their useful life. It is a good way to make sure that you have herbs to use all year round.

Dried herbs are not only for teas and bath implements. They are also useful in casting spells.

Uses of Herbs for Magick

-Bath – Make a sachet, like a string-tied hessian bag. Add dried or fresh herbs and put the bag in your bath water for a refreshing ritual healing bath.

-Oils – Premade oils are available, but you can create your own by putting fresh herbs in oil. Steep the herbs for several days, then strain.

-Incense – You can burn herbs as a ritual incense, as well as for its scent and different properties.

-Teas – Herbs offer different qualities that are ideal for teas. You can seep herbs in hot water to make fresh tea, or you can buy loose leaf bags that come with a strainer.

-Spells and charms – Various herbs are used as ingredients in various charms and spells because they add potency to the works.

Herbs Used in Wicca

Following are some of the herbs used by Wiccans for various purposes such as making spells. Also included are the herbs' properties and uses.

Bay Leaves

Planet: Sun

Element: Fire

Gender: Masculine

Uses: For protection, and to prevent being jinxed or hexed.

How to use:

• Keep it under your pillow to attract prophetic dreams.

- Scatter them on the floor, then sweep. This will provide protection.

- Carry it to keep evil at bay.

Echinacea

Planet: Mars

Element: Earth

Gender: Masculine

Uses: For strengthening powers

How to use:

- Put it in a vase and keep it in your household, this will attract prosperity to your home.

- Carry it. It will help see you through financial difficulties.

- Include it in a spell. This will enhance the spell's effectiveness.

Mint

Planet: Venus

Element: Water

Gender: Female

Uses: For enhancing vitality, energy, and communication

How to use:

• Place in boiling water and inhale the leaves. This will help relieve headaches.

• Use it as a floor wash. This will invite good fortune and happiness into your household.

Chamomile

Planet: Sun

Element: Water

Gender: Masculine

Uses: For attracting love and for good luck; also used for prosperity wishes, attracting money, and as a prosperity amulet

How to use:

•   Use it as tea; it has great relaxing properties.

•   Use it as an incense to help in meditation. It also promotes good sleep quality.

•   Use it to wash your hair and face, or add it to your bath water. Chamomile helps attract love.

•   Use it to break curses that were cast on you.

•   Use it for bathing children. It will protect them from the evil eye.

Lavender

Planet: Mercury

Element: Air

Gender: Male

Uses: For love, peace, purification, and sleep

How to use:

•   Burn it as an incense while meditating. This will keep you relaxed. It will also help open your mind.

•   Carry a few lavender sprigs or hang them in your home to attract love into your life.

•   Uşe it in bath spells and sleep pillows.

Rosemary

Planet: Sun

Element: Fire

Gender: Male

Uses: For memory spells; once known as 'elf leaf' used to avoid witches.

How to use:

- Use it for lust and love potions and incenses.

- Use it as a tea. It will keep your mind alert.

Bear in mind that herbs have inherent powers. Thus, it is important that you take the proper caution when using them. Make sure to use herbs safely, and in the proper amount, in particular, when ingesting them, or using them on children and pregnant women.

Herbal Spells for Beginners

Herbal Dream Spells

Psychic Dreams Herb Pillow

This classic dream spell involves the use of a tiny pillow of herbs. This is because it tends to work best that way. The simple pillow comprises of two stitched-together fabric pieces. It need not be fancy, for so long as the stitching and weave are tight enough to prevent loose herbs from falling out.

What you'll need:

1 or 2 tablespoons of the following:

- Mugwort

- Angelica

- Cinnamon

- Wormwood

- Rowan

- Lemon Balm

How to do it:

It does not have to be the exact blend of the above ingredients. But, you must have at least 3 of them in your herbal mix. Make sure that one of the ingredients is mugwort. The spell won't work without it.

Mix all the ingredients together, then stuff them into the pillow. You may have to wait for a few nights for the spell to take effect. So, don't expect the results to be immediate.

After 3 nights, start to record your dreams. You'll be surprised by the changes. Only time will tell how predictive they turn out to be. Continue to record for about a month. Take a break and set the pillow aside. Check if your dreams have revealed anything to you. After one month, you can start again with a new pillow.

Soul Mate Dreaming

This spell is what a lot of people are looking for. After all, it's no secret that many people want to meet their soul mate in their dreams.

The spell will bring the dreams you want: your soul mate, to be specific. But, bear in mind that dreams may be symbolic. They may not present to you a clear snapshot of your soul mate's face. You may need to interpret your dreams. So, be ready!

What you'll need:

- A sheet of pink paper

- Lemon juice

- Cinnamon oil

- Patchouli oil

How to do it:

Jot down your name on the sheet of paper. Put a drop of the lemon juice and each of the oils, then wait until everything is completely dry. Fold the paper in half for four times. If you weren't able to prepare the oils, you can instead use the dry herbs. All you have to do is rub the herbs on the pink paper. But, don't expect it to be as potent.

Tuck the folded paper underneath your pillow. In 4 nights, you will have a dream that will point the way to your soul mate. The dream may not identify you soul mate, but it may give a clue about the circumstances that will lead to your encounter.

General Purpose Herbal Spells

Potion to Unleash Your Power

This general purpose spell will help bring out the best in your – just when you need it! This comes in handy during important exams, job interviews, and even when you are about to launch a new business. It will give you the much-needed energy boost!

What you'll need:

• Pure water (preferably rainwater, but distilled water will work fine)

• A few pinches of ginger and ground allspice

• 1 piece of lemon

• Vanilla extract

• 1 red marker

• 1 sheet of white paper

• Red ribbon or yarn

How to do it:

On a sheet of white paper, draw a large-sized pentacle. Place a glass of water at the center. Add a bit of ginger and allspice to the water, followed by the vanilla extract (3 drops).

Cut the lemon in half as you say the following words:

By this potion I ask,

Give me the power to do my task

Herbs and fruit, and the color red

Down this path, lead the spell.

Now, squeeze the lemon into the glass. Wrap the yarn around your glass for several times. Tie in a knot.

Focus on the reason you are doing the spell as you let the potion sit for several minutes. This will help transfer energy into the potion. Using your right hand, pick up the glass. Take a good sip. You need not finish everything.

Leave the glass untouched until the event you have been preparing for has passed. This could be a job interview or a big exam. Then, pour whatever is remaining in the glass into the earth. Do not throw it down the drain!

Third Eye Draft

The spell and potion will help you open your third eye. When this happens, you can expect to welcome more psychic experiences to your life. This is not a medicinal recipe, but a magickal one. Thus, you shouldn't expect any weird, drug-related hallucinations from the concoction.

What you'll need:

• Access to heat source (a stovetop is fine, but not a microwave oven)

• Dried mugwort

• Pure water

- Dried rosemary

- 1 white feather

- 3 pieces of moonstone

How to do it:

Heat up a small-sized pot of water on the stove. Add a pinch of rosemary and 1 teaspoon of dried mugwort. Bring everything to a simmer.

Drop the crystals, one moonstone at a time. Stir exactly 3 times in clockwise direction.

Get the feather and make it touch the water surface. Then, make it touch your forehead. Allow the brew to simmer for a few minutes more. Set it aside to cool down.

Pour the brew into a cup. Have a drink. Make sure not to choke on the pieces of moonstone, but you should not leave them in the cup. Expect your third eye to begin to open. In no time, you will be ready for some psychic experience and inspiration.

** Bear in mind that the mugwort will trigger some physical effects on you. After all, most herbs do. Refrain from using the potion if you are nursing or pregnant.

Herbal Love Spells

Lemon Love Spell

If you want to get back together with your ex, this is the spell that will help you achieve your goal. The best part is, it is very easy to do.

What you'll need:

- 1 fresh lemon

- 1 small piece of paper (preferably pink)

- A length of red ribbon or yarn

How to do it:

Write your name as well as the name of your ex on the sheet of paper. Slice the lemon open. Cut it in half as evenly as possible. Fold the paper in a way that the names are touching. Put it between two lemon halves. Hold the lemon together by tying the red yarn around it. While you are doing it, imagine you and your ex are back together. Imagine how happy you would feel when that happens.

Put the bound lemon inside the freezer. Hide it in the back so no one will notice it. Within a month, expect to welcome your ex back into your life.

Triple Knot Love Spell

Typically, knot spells don't require too many supplies, and are often easy to do. The knot binds your intention as you perform the spell.

What you'll need:

- Patchouli oil

- Ylang ylang oil

- At least 2' feet of red ribbon

How to do it:

Put a drop or two of each of the oils in your palms, then rub them together. Anoint it by running your fingers along the ribbon.

Because you will need to tie 3 knots, make sure there is good spacing along the length of the ribbon.

Say one line of the spell as you make a knot. Say the first line for the first knot, the second line for the second knot, and the third line for the last knot:

With one knot, my love comes

With two knots, it will be true

With three knots, let it be done.

After completing the third knot, loop the ribbon around your bedside lamp, doorknob, or bed post in your bedroom. But, don't tie it as it may create an extra knot that may spoil the spell.

Herbal Love Box

The combined scent of herbs and petals can bring love in the air. How much more when you use them in a spell? The love will be a hundredfold. As much as possible, perform the spell under a full moon.

What you'll need:

- Rose petals

- Lavender buds

- Damiana root

- 1 pinch of ground cinnamon

- Chopped vanilla bean

- 1 piece of clear or rose quartz

- 1 piece of white paper

- 1 small lidded bowl or box

How to do it:

The size of the bowl or box you have will determine the amount of each herb you will need. You must have a sufficient amount of the herb mix to fill up the bowl.

You can play with the proportions. Just make sure that all the ingredients in the list are there.

Once you have gathered all the materials, mix the herbs and flowers together. Fill the lower half of the bowl.

Get the piece of paper and write down the 5 qualities that you want your new partner to have. Make sure to write personality traits, and not physical qualities. Fold the paper, making sure that it will fit into the bowl.

Now, fill up the rest of the bowl with the herbs, with the crystal nestled at the top of the herbs. Close the lid.

Every night, remove the lid of the bowl, and sniff the contents. This is to refresh your memory about your quest to find true love.

Love Pouch

A spell pouch is one of the best types of magick to have because it is quite portable. This way, you can have some magick with you at all times. Beware, though. This spell might make you quite popular among cats!

What you'll need:

•   1 small pink pouch (preferably made of silk or cotton)

•   Jasmine flowers

•   4 pieces of pink or white candles

•   Catnip

•   1 fire-proof pot or cauldron

•   1 pen

•   1 piece of paper

How to do it:

Set the 4 candles on your altar. Make sure they're at the 4 cardinal directions (east, west, north, and south.), and the cauldron is at the center.

Put the jasmine and catnip in the cauldron. Get the piece of paper and jot down all the things you want in a relationship and in a partner. Sign it, then fold the paper. Put it inside the cauldron. Light it up.

Only the piece of paper will burn. The herbs will not. While the paper is burning, say the following words:

By the power of words and flame, bring love to me.

Repeat the words again and again. Don't stop until the piece of paper is completely burned out.

Stir the remaining ashes and mix them with the herbs. Pour everything into the bag. Tie the bag tightly to close. Make sure to carry the pouch with your around at all times.

Classic Love Potion No. 9

Among all types of Wiccan magick, love potions are perhaps the most popular. This is because this type of spell is what we often see in Disney movies and classic fairy tales. In a love potion, the spell is completed once the potion is ingested.

But, in some cases, the term love potion is used not just for drinking potions, but for any type of liquid as well. This may include an oil blend for a bath spell.

The Classic Love Potion No. 9 is another example. Obviously, it is based on #9, a magickal number. The potion spell is easy to concoct, and while there are many ingredients, these are all readily available.

What you'll need:

- 9 fresh basil leaves

- 9 oz. of sweet red wine

- 9 whole cloves

- 9 apple seeds

- 9 fresh red rose petals

- 9 drops of fresh vanilla extract

- 9 drops of apple juice

- 9 drops of strawberry juice

- 9 small-sized pieces of ginseng root

- 9 pink candles

- 1 large-sized cooking pot

- 1 small glass bottle with stopper

- 1 cheesecloth or fine strainer

How to do it:

Light up the candles around the space where you plan to make the potion. This could be the kitchen. Mix all ingredients together in the pot. Stir over low heat setting as you say the following words:

Let the person who drinks the wine

Shower me with divine love

Love potion No. 9,

Let the love be mine forever.

Bring the concoction to a low simmer. Allow it to heat for 9 minutes more. Remove the pot from the heat. Allow it to cool. As it cools down, recite the names of the 9 love goddesses out loud:

Venus

Ishtar

Astarte

Nephthys,

Aphrodite

Hathor

Freya

Inanna

Arianrhod

Strain the fresh potion to get rid of the remaining bits and pieces. Pour into a bottle with stopper. Put it in the refrigerator until you need to use it.

Give it to someone you love or add to their drink. This will give a tremendous boost of romantic magick!

Aphrodesia Passion Tea

If you want to put your lover in a nice romantic mood, then a warm cup of this love potion tea will do the trick. If you ask me, the Aphrodesia Passion Tea is more like a passion potion, and not so much of a love potion.

What you'll need:

- 1 pinch of thyme

- 1 pinch of rosemary

- 1 pinch of nutmeg

- 1 pinch of damiana

- 3 rose petals

- 3 mint leaves

- 2 teaspoons of black tea leaves

- 3 small-sized pieces of lemon zest

How to do it:

Boil 3 cups of water, then add all the ingredients. Allow the mixture to steep in a teapot. Focus on erotic thoughts as you let the tea boil for several minutes. Pour the tea in to cups. Add generous amounts of honey to sweeten.

When using a love potion, bear in mind that it has limits. Making another person fall in love with you can be difficult and tricky. Spells may not always work, especially if the person you are trying to win over isn't interested in you at all, in the first place.

Seeds of Love

While you may not really plant the seeds of love on the ground, the Seeds of Love charm can encourage love to bloom.

What you'll need:

- 9 sunflower seeds

- 9 dried corn kernels

- 9 dried beans

- 9 dry chamomile buds

- 9 grains of barley

- 9 whole cloves

- Some rose oil

- Red ribbon

- 1 glass bottle w/ stopper (make sure it's big enough to hold all seeds, but not too big to leave a lot of empty space on top)

How to do it:

Drop the seeds, one at a time, into the bottle. Be patient. Don't rush as it may affect the spell. As you drop the seeds, say the following words:

Spices and seeds, give me the power

It's time to make a flower for my love life

As the moon rises in the sky

The charm will cause my wishes to fly.

Once the bottle is filled up, put 9 drops on top, then seal the bottle with the stopper. Avoid shaking the bottle. You must allow the oil go down on its own – from the top until it reaches the bottom.

Tie the ribbon in a bow and place it around the bottle. Take the bottle to an area that is quiet, and where it will not be disturbed.

Wait for the full moon. By then, you should experience some exciting action in your love life.

Your Heart Be Mine Bath Spell

You can win over someone's heart as you immerse yourself in this love spell completely. This is one spell that is easy to perform and only requires a few easy to find things.

What you'll need:

- 2 white candles

- 2 pink candles

- 1 piece of paper

- 1 red marker

- Some ylang ylang or Jasmin oil

How to do it:

Before starting work on the spell, prepare a hot bath for yourself. Light up the candles at the 4 corners of your bath tub.

Using the red marker, draw a large-sized hat on the piece of paper. Write your and your prospective lover's name at the center. Draw a bigger heart around the first heart (make sure to draw the larger heart after you have written your names.)

Rub a drop of the oil into every corner of the paper. Fold the paper into quarters. Pick it up, and hold it in your hands. Say the two names you wrote aloud for a few times. Without unfolding the paper, tear it into several small pieces. Drop the paper pieces into the bath water.

Get in the bath tub. Try to dissolve the paper by stirring the water around. Rub the pieces of paper on your body as you continue to soak in the water. Wait until the paper is broken down completely in the water before getting out of the tub.

Wait for signs that the person you want is starting to fall for you. It will happen in time if the person had at least some initial interest in you. Just be patient.

Passion on Your Doorstep

This spell is interesting because of the hot pepper ingredient. But, I can assure you that it is totally Wiccan.

What you'll need:

- 3 cups of rain water

- Black peppercorns

- Dried rosemary

- 3 drops of lavender oil

- Dried pieces of orris root

- 3 drops of hot pepper sauce

How to do it:

The herbal ingredients don't require precise measurements. 2 to 3 pinches of each herb would be enough. What's important is to use equal amounts for all the herbal ingredients.

Mix all ingredients together in one bowl. Stir well. As you do this, focus on attracting passion and love into your life.

Use your fingers to sprinkle the mix around your front door. Make sure to distribute it well. Don't pour everything in only a one or two spots.

Once done scattering the mixture, wash your hands thoroughly. Wait for love to come looking for you. It should not take long.

Bell of Beauty

Don't let the name mislead you. The Bell of Beauty is not merely a beauty spell. More importantly, it will make you look quite attractive to the one person you want to notice you.

While you can direct the spell on anyone you wish, it will be most effective on a person who is meant for you. If the spell gets the attention of someone else, other than the person you are eyeing, the Universe might be telling you something. So, keep your eyes open!

What you'll need:

- 1 length each of white, pink, and red ribbon

- A handful of rose petals (dry or fresh)

- 1 saucer or shallow dish

- Vanilla oil or extract

- 1 silver bell

How to do it:

Fill up the dish with the rose petals. Tie the ribbons on the bell's handle. Say the first line of the spell's words as you tie the first ribbon, the second line as you tie the second ribbon, and the third line as you tie the third ribbon:

The pealing of the bell, the sounding of the tone,

It is about time that our love grows,

Open (your target person's name)'s eyes to see only me.

Using your finger, rub some vanilla along the bell's rim. Say the 3 lines one more time, ringing the bell as you say each line.

Place the bell on top of the petals. Each morning, upon waking up, ring the bell. This will activate the Bell of Beauty spell for the day. In a matter of days, the person you want to be with will begin to notice you.

Flower Petal Love Charm

This spell needs various kinds of flowers. This can be hard, particularly if you want to cast the spell right in the middle of winter. Fresh flowers are ideal, but if it is not possible, then dried flowers will suffice.

What you'll need:

• 1 small-sized, thin pink bag

• Petals from at least 5 of the following flowers: rose, lavender, chamomile, daffodil, carnation, geranium, poppy, and honeysuckle

• 5 apple seeds

Note: You need a bag mad of a type of gauze or mesh. This way, you can see what's inside (the flowers). It will also allow some air to flow through the bag. If you don't have one, you can often find it in craft stores' wedding favor section. You also need to prepare around a tablespoon for every kind of petal.

How to do it:

Drop the petals, one at a time, into the bag. This may be a tedious process, but there is no other way to do it if you want the spell to work. Each time you drop a petal, say: He loves me and He loves me not in the next. Continue to say the classic line until you drop the last petal into the bag, but make sure you end up with He loves me.

Once done, add the 5 apple seeds. Tightly tie the bag to seal it. Hang it inside your bathroom. Make sure it is somewhere safe. Leave it there for less than a month. Make sure not to leave it longer than that. You will hopefully find a new romance within that period of time.

Blush of Blooming Love

You can turn your friendship into a more meaningful relationship with the help of this spell.

What you'll need:

- 1 pink carnation

- 1 red carnation

- 1 white carnation

- 1 glass vase

- 1 piece of white paper (about the size of a stamp)

- 1 teaspoon of red food coloring

- 1 red pen or marker

Note: All the flowers must be fresh, with their stems intact.

How to do it:

Fill up the glass vase with water. Put 7 drops of the food coloring.

On the stamp-sized piece of paper, draw the image of a small pentacle. Fold the paper, and drop it in the water-filled vase. Snip off the bottom of the flower stems, about an inch each. Drop the snipped stem portions into the vase. Then, recite the following:

Pink, red, and white,

May your heart heed

Take the blush of blooming love

With power from above.

Now, using your index finger, touch each flower at the center. Say the words again as you do this.

Leave the vase and the flowers in a place where there is enough sunlight, but make sure it is not too hot. In a few days, you'll notice the red dye has moved up into the flowers. It is now starting to give them a red tinge. You will notice it more in the white carnation.

Once you see that the red dye has given its color to the white carnation's petals, cut of a big part of the stem. Bring the flower with you at all times during the day. Your target person must see it so the spell can work.

Herbal Marriage Spells

A marriage spell can help elevate your relationship to a higher level. This is useful if your partner is having second thoughts about making a commitment.

But, remember that forcing someone into a relationship when that person isn't ready yet can lead to a disaster.

Having said that, a bit of magickal push won't hurt, either!

Following are some Wiccan marriage spells that you can use to give your partner a little nudge, and help push your relationship to something more serious.

The Marriage Moon Spell

The marriage spell is best done when the moon is full. To be specific, you must find a place where you have a clear view of the moon. This could be inside or outside you home. If the sky is overcast, do it some other time.

What you'll need:

- 1 fresh with rose

- 1 silver ring (it doesn't have to be real silver)

- A few pinches of dried damiana, lemon verbena, and yarrow

- 1 small white dish

How to do it:

Before casting the spell, put the ring in the bowl with the herbs. Leave everything untouched for 1 whole day. Come back during the night when there is a full moon.

Stand up to face the moon. Hold the ring up in a way that you can see the moon's glowing face through the center of the ring. Then, say the following words aloud:

Bring the bond that I desire

My love will never tire

By this full moon's light,

Bring marriage to me very soon.

Hold the rose up in a way that the flower is covering the face of the moon. Repeat the words. Put down the ring below the rose's stem. It should sit at the flower base.

Place the ring and flower into the herb bowl, then say the words for the last time. Don't touch anything until the night of the next full moon. By then, you should start to see sights that your spell is working.

Herbal Lust Spells

Light My Fire

You can use the spell to kindle another person's lust, or even your own – if you need a lift in this department, that is.

What you'll need:

- 1 red human figure candle (in your target's gender; if you can't find a gender-specific human figure candle, a plain red candle would be alright; just carve the male or female symbol into the candle first)

- Tabasco sauce or hot chili oil

- 3 whole cloves

How to do it:

Anoint the whole candle with some vanilla oil. Use your fingers to do it. On one side of the candle, push the cloves in. If necessary, use a pointed object to create holes in the wax first. Any technique that works for you is fine.

Rub the candle's bottom half with chili oil. Then, set up the candle. Light it up.

While the candle light is flickering, focus on the flame. Say the following words:

Light up the fire,

Bring out the flame

Let the passion grow

Something that is hard to tame.

Repeat the words 4 times more, while the candle continues to burn. Imagine your target person getting consumed by the flames. Then, repeat the words once more.

Allow the candle to burn out – all the way – on its own. Expect your wish to come true very soon!

No Strings Attached

Are you looking for a great sexual encounter, but without the usual emotional commitment that comes with one? This is the spell to use if you want to find that ideal sexual partner that you desire – with no strings attached! But first, you need to set up your bedroom with the necessary materials.

What you'll need:

- 2 pieces of hot peppers (fresh and whole)

- 2 cinnamon incense sticks

How to do it:

Light up the incense sticks on opposite sides of your room. Give them a few minutes to smolder, and spread the smoke throughout the space. Concentrate on your intentions of finding a willing sexual partner, who, like you, is not looking for a serious relationship or romance – but sex and sex alone! Ask the Universe to bring that person to you.

Put 1 of the hot peppers under 1 side of the mattress. Place the other hot pepper on the opposite side. At night, sleep on one side of your bed. Do this until the spell works, and someone that you find desirable comes over to occupy the other side of the bed!

Herbal Friendship Spells

A friendship spell is similar to a love spell, only a bit lighter. It is meant to develop a relationship with another person – with a little help from magick! While this type of spell is not as common as love spells, they can be quite helpful too. This is true, in particular, if you're not a sociable person by nature.

Find a Friend Charm

Carry the small charm bag anytime you want to find a new friend, someone you have a lot in common with.

What you'll need:

- 1 square piece of white silk (such as a hankie)

- 1 pink ribbon or yarn

- 3 silver coins (not necessarily real silver; standard dimes or nickels would do just fine)

- Honeysuckle fragrance or oil

- 1 mint leaf (preferably fresh, and not dried)

How to do it:

Lay the white cloth down. Place the mint leaf at the center. Rub each coin with a drop of oil, then place them in one pile on the mint leaf. Fold up the corners of the white silk. Make a small bundle by tying the yarn around it.

Leave it in a windowsill for two nights. The current moon phase doesn't matter. Just leave the bundle undisturbed. After two days, get the charm and carry it with you everywhere you go.

Smooth the Waters

This spell is ideal for use when you want to mend or improve a friendship that is currently undergoing rough sailing.

What you'll need:

- 1 large-sized bowl (make sure it's not plastic)

- A pinch of salt

- A pinch of rosemary

- 1 key

- 1 piece of string (around 1' long)

How to do it:

Fill the large bowl with water. Add a pinch each of rosemary and salt. Use your finger to stir the mixture.

Make sure to get some water ripples. Then, say the following words:

Calm the waters for me and my friend,

Let our troubles end finally.

As you watch the bowl of water, sway the key above the surface, then say the words again and again until the water becomes still.

For three days, wear the key like a necklace. Make sure that you exert enough effort in fixing whatever problems may be plaguing your friendship. The spell will help calm down any tension that may be existing.

Chapter 5: Moon Spells

You can always perform Wiccan spells whenever you need to – it doesn't matter what phase the moon is currently in. But, there are practitioners who believe that it is more effective to time your spells with lunar cycles. This way, the moon can infuse her mysterious power into your spells.

In Wicca, the moon is sacred. She has a deep energetic influence on our inner world. The moon's emotions radiate down to earth, making us feel the same emotions she is currently feeling. She is beguiling and bewitching. In a matter of just 29.5 days, she can make a complete switch from heightened energy to yearning.

The moon's phases offer the perfect setting for a wide variety of spells. Thus, it is not surprising that casting spells that align with the cycles of the moon is common in Wicca.

The New Moon

The new moon is the period when the moon is not visible from the Earth. The sun blocks the moon's reflections. But, lunar energy is ripe and conducive for new beginnings.

This is the perfect time to make plans, adopt new habits, start new projects, and move on from things that are keeping you from improving. The new moon is also a great time to introduce changes, growth, and development into your life.

In Wicca, the new moon is the time for purification and cleansing spells. During this time, it is also ideal to cast spells for luck. These include spells to gain enough money for your monthly needs, or just to make a wish.

To make a new moon wish, go outdoors at the start of the new moon cycle, then look up to the moon. You can create a simple ritual like turning around 3 times, lighting a candle, or giving thanks to the moon. Then, you send your wish to the moon.

Waxing Moon

The moon's energy builds up with the coming of the waxing moon. The moon phase lasts for about 7 days at the end of the new moon. During the waxing moon phase, the moon supports creation. This is because she is in the stage of growth, and is building up to her full capacity.

At this time, the plans and projects that were made during the new moon are now taking shape. It is the time to proceed with all your plans. The waxing moon phase is the ideal time for absorption, taking vitamins, learning, and nurturing your magickal garden – in case you have one. But, you have to beware! This is because during this lunar phase, you may be prone to over-doing things. It is therefore important to maintain sobriety.

Spells done during the waxing phase often bring positive results. Thus, if there's something new you want to have in your life, now is the right time to wish for it. This may be friendship, love, fertility, money, etc.

The phase is also a great time to work on moon spells or meditate with the moon. It is sure to provide you with new insights.

Full Moon

The full moon phase happens around 14 days from the full moon phase. This is the time when the moon has reached her peak. Her energy level is high, and beams down on the Earth below. Her energy amplifies our emotions – for better or worse. Thus, depending on the energy that dominates at present it can either be a tricky or a wonderful time!

This is the best time to finalize your plans and projects. This is to prepare for the more sober energy that is about to come. It is also a great time to meditate on your inner-world and your life in general. Also, dreams may be more profound at this time.

It is a good idea to appreciate what you currently have in your life, as well as to be mindful of things that you no longer have any use for.

When the moon has just past its fullest stage, the time is ripe for spells that are meant to banish addictions, file for divorce, help with decision-making, manage your stress and emotions, and provide protection. The full moon is also helpful for building knowledge, as well as for creating and sharing a calming environment. It also helps in meditation and facilitates communication.

In other words, the full moon is a busy season! If you have something that needs extra power, like an illness or a grave home problem, the full moon offers the perfect setting for casting a moon spell to address the issue.

Wiccans believe that the full moon is the best time to cast protection spells, as well as spells that will help enhance your psychic abilities, and perform rituals for protection and divination. Never forget to charge your tools and crystals during the full moon phase.

Waning Moon

Around 7 days after the full moon, the waning moon phase starts. As the moon withdraws, the energy of the waning moon looks softer. During this time, life will tend to slow down, as if an invisible brake is stepped on.

This is the ideal time for meditation, and for casting cleansing spells. It is also a good time for creating banishing and reversing spells.

Wiccan Moon Spells

There are Wiccan spells that are cast to coincide with specific phases of the moon. This helps harness lunar power, and boost the energy of the spell or ritual. Moon spells can be performed for specific purposes, or simply to attract blessings into your life.

If you need to cast a full moon spell, for example, it is not necessary to perform the spell right on the instance of a full moon. This is because you can harness the moon's energy 1 day before and after the actual full moon. This practically gives you a three-day window that you can use to plan and perform you spell.

The window is even longer for full moon love spells. This is because you can cast your love spell two days before and after the actual night of the full moon. The 4-day window is longer than what most other Wiccan love spells allow.

Having said that, it is best to perform your spell as close as possible to your target moon phase.

Sweet Apple Enchantment Spell

Ever wonder why some great Wiccan spells require a lock of hair? The answer is simple. The hair is one powerful way to associate your target person to the spell. This is what this spell aims to achieve.

What you'll need:

- 1 red apple

- Several strands of your target lover's hair

- Several strands of your own hair

- Honey

- 1 length of red yarn or ribbon

How to do it:

Cut the apple across the middle, sideways. This way, you can easily see the star-shape formed by the apple seeds.

Spread some honey on one half of the apple. Get the hair strands, and braid or twist them together.

Place the twisted/braided hair between the apple halves. Using the ribbon, tie the halved fruit back together. Make sure it is tight.

Bury the tied apple outdoors or inside a large-sized flower pot inside your home. Either option will do, but burying it outside your home is better.

Within a short period of time, you will notice your target beginning to show a strong attraction to you. It is then up to you to help the relationship flourish. After all, the seeds have been planted!

Waning Moon Banishing Spell

You can use this spell if there is something in your life at present that you want to banish. This may include a toxic person or an assigned task at work that you do not want to complete.

What you'll need:

- 2' of cord (ideally black)

- Lemongrass essential oil

- 1 pen

- 1 piece of paper

How to do it:

Identify something in your life that you want to banish for good. On the piece of paper, write a word that will symbolize or describe what you want to get rid of.

Tie a loose knot on one end of the black cord. Look through the knot's loop and read what you wrote down. Tighten the knot slowly.

Visualize how the knot is starting to bind the negative energy to the cord. Put a drop of the essential oil on the knot. Then, say the words:

I bind and banish you forever from my life.

Tie another knot, and then another, and stop only after you have made 6 knots. You can then keep the cord somewhere safe, or you can dispose of it, together with the piece of paper. What you do with the cord and paper will depend on what feels right to you.

Two Halves Made Whole

One powerful talisman you can use for a spell to reunite you with your ex is a picture of the two of you together. The spell is best done when the moon is slowly turning into a full moon. This is called the waxing moon phase.

What you'll need:

- A picture of you and your loved one together

- 1 red candle

- 1 black candle

- 1 athame (sharp ritual knife or dagger)

- 1 charcoal tablet

- Coriander seeds

** Note: You will need to cut the picture in half. Thus, if it is important for you to keep it intact, just make a copy for the spell. Even if you use the copy, the spell should still work well. Also, if an athame is not available, you can just use a regular, clean kitchen knife. But, never use a pair of scissors.

How to do it:

Light up the two candles. Position the red candle on your right side, and the black on your left. Place the charcoal between the candles, on top of a heat-proof surface. Light it up.

Sprinkle some coriander seeds over the charcoal. Wait for the seeds to begin smoking. You may open a window to let the smoke out.

Slice the photo in two using the athame. Make sure to cut the people (you and your lover) in the picture apart. Then, say the following:

Rent and torn,

Forlorn love,

Hearts apart,

Hearts broken.

Hold the 2 pieces of photos up. Let the coriander smoke flow between them as you utter the words again.

Lay down the photo pieces together in a way that they overlap. No need to be too precise for this step.

Drip some black wax on them. Make sure the wax binds them. Once bound by the black wax, drop red box on top. Once the wax cools down, the halved picture must stick together.

Hold up the mended photo to the smoke. Now, say the following:

By the morning,

Love is reborn,

Pieced back together,

Now and forever.

Put out the flames on the candles. Leave the photo between the candles on the altar until your loved one has come back to you.

Waxing Moon Spell for Focusing

You can use this spell to enhance your concentration, as well as to learn new insights.

What you'll need:

- 1 yellow candle

- Something sharp to use for carving symbols on the candle

- 1 small piece of paper

- 1 pen

- 1 flame-proof dish

How to do it:

Carve a symbol to represent wisdom and concentration on the candle. Light up the candle, focus on the flame, and center yourself.

Picture the light slowly filling your head, helping make it focused, alert, and clear. Then, say the following words:

Lively and bright is the flame

My mind, I will to be the same

My disorganized thoughts disappear

The moments of clarity are so near

I will be attentive as it burns.

As I work, I focus on everything

I'll study hard and focus well

Success is my due reward.

Now, draw a symbol to represent disorganized thoughts on the small piece of paper. As the paper burns, visualize the very same thing happening to your distracting thoughts. Work within the circle. Make sure to keep the candle lit up as you proceed. Once you are done with your work, put the flame out, then close your circle.

Love on the Wind Spell

As the name of the spell suggests, it is another one of those that use the Air element to find the love of your life.

What you'll need:

- 1 small bell

- 1 sprig of yarrow

- 1 sprig of rosemary

- A few strands of your hair

- string

How to do it:

You can use either fresh or dry herbs. But, you have to make sure they're in "sprig form" and not ground up.

On a full moon, assemble your materials for the spell charm. Get a string and on one end, tie your hair, herbs, and bell in a knot. Tie three knots along the length of the rest of the string. Make sure the knots have equal spacing.

By midnight, go outside your house. Tie the string to a tree in a way that the items tied to the charm are dangling. You may hide it in the branches, but make sure the dangling items are not bound too tightly, and can still move about.

In no time, the spell charm will begin to draw love into your life. This can be as soon as the following day. Keep your eyes open for signs of a new person in your life.

Full Moon Wish Spell

You can harness lunar energy for any purpose through this wish spell. If you want to welcome something unexpected to your life, this is the right spell for you.

What you'll need:

- Pure water

- 1 clear jar (not less than 1 pint)

- 1 silver coin

- 1 bell

- 1 silver or white candle

How to do it:

Make sure to perform the spell on a clear night when you have a good view of the moon. Do it outside your home, if possible, but you can just settle for the window if going out is not an option at the moment.

Fill your jar with pure water, then light up the candle. Do this somewhere near the space you plan on performing the spell. Just sit and stare at the moon for several minutes to enjoy its bright light.

Drop the silver coin into the jar. Allow the water to settle down. Wait until it's all clear and smooth again. Sit down in a way that you can see the moon's reflection in the water will seem to rest on the coin. Move around, if necessary, to find the best place for this.

Stare at the coin with the moon's reflection on it. As you do this, ring the bell 3 times. Say your wish aloud. If you do not have a specific wish in mind, you can just request the moon to give you good fortune in general.

If you are performing the spell outdoors, bring everything inside your home, but do not take the coin out of the jar, at least until the night of the next full moon. Or, when you feel that you have already gotten your wish.

Salt of the Earth Spell

By casting this spell, you harness the power of the full moon to help you welcome a new love into your life. The spell requires lighting up a fire, so you may want to find a place where you can safely set up the fire. It is best done outdoors, but using a woodstove, fireplace, or a cast-iron cauldron is fine.

What you'll need:

- 1 or 2 handfuls of coarse salt

- 1 or 2 handfuls of dried rose petals

- Space to safely start a fire

How to do it:

The spell will take 3 nights to complete. It starts on the eve of the official date of the full moon.

First, light up a small fire using any kind of wood. Stand near the fire. Throw in some coarse salt as you say the following:

Let his/her (depending on your target's gender) heart burn only for me

Kindled under the moonlight,

Let his heart burn only for me

Bring him soon to me.

Toss some rose petals in, then repeat the words. Allow the fire to continue burning for a few more minutes. Or, if you prefer, you can now put out the fire.

Perform the ritual for the succeeding two nights. Your new love should come knocking in your heart before the night of the next full moon.

Venus Love Charm

Full moon love spells often involve the colors red or pink. This spell is one of the rare exceptions. This time, we'll use the energy from a different color. But, rest assured that the spell will be effective just the same. As long as you keep the faith and focus all your energy into the spell, there's no reason it will not be successful.

What you'll need:

- 1 new silver coin

- 4 rose quartz pieces

- 1 purple candle

- 1 square piece of silk

How to do it:

The spell is best done on a full moon night. First, lay down the silk on your altar. Place the candle at the center. Secure it with a candle holder. Note that wax might drip on the silk; thus, it is better not to use a valuable or important piece of silk for the spell.

Place the silver coin on the candle's southern side, but still on the silk cloth. If you are not sure about where the south is, you can use a compass for the purpose.

Put the quartz crystals on each corner of the cloth. Light up your candle, then say the spell words 4 times. Touch 1 crystal for each time you recite the following words:

From the Earth's four corners

Bring to me my true love.

Visualize the light coming out of the candle, then dispersing into the world. The light is trying to find and connect with your true love. You must not imagine or picture any particular person, if possible.

Allow the candle to burn throughout the night, then gather the coin and crystals in a bundle using the silk cloth. Leave the bundle on the altar.

Money Wish Spell

You can cast this spell anytime you need financial help. You only have to use your magickal creation power and visualization skills. For best results, I recommend that you perform this spell on a Sunday, Thursday, or Friday of a waxing moon or full moon.

What you'll need:

- 1 special coin or lucky charm

- Powerful visualization skills

How to do it:

Determine how much you need. Imagine yourself having tons of wealth and riches. Now, imagine yourself getting the money you need. Your intention helps you supercharge your special coin. This way, your ability to create magick will work faster, and the Universe will respond positively to your request sooner.

Continue to meditate on your wish. Think about what will happen if you have the money you need. How much better will your life be with the financial windfall?

Now, hold on to your special coin or lucky charm, then say the words of the spell:

Gold and silver, return to me

By the powers of 300 times 3

The money I need will be mine to keep

Make your way, and find me right away.

After completing the chant, thank the Universe and the goddess for blessing you the money you need.

Make sure to carry the coin with you at all times. In no time, you will receive the money you need.

Money Rock

The spell is best done during the moon's waxing phase. It will bring you the money you need to address you current financial woes.

What you'll need:

- 1 green candle

- Some green paint

- 1 rock with an almost square shape

How to do it:

Charge the candle with money-drawing energy. Picture yourself receiving and enjoying all the money you need.

Once you are ready to proceed, light up the candle. As the candle flame continues to glow, paint some money symbols on the square-shaped rock. You can use currency symbols like $, £, €, and ¥, as well as other symbols that remind you of money.

While painting the symbols, focus on how the rock will deliver the money you need. Wait for 7 minutes, then put out the candle's flame.

Each day, light up the candle for 7 minutes. Do this until the money you need comes your way.

Prosperity Moon Spell

This spell for money and prosperity is best performed during the waxing moon phase, specifically on a Thursday or Sunday. The lunar energy will help you get the financial blessing you need.

What you'll need:

•   1 cauldron that contains burning charcoal

•   1 cup of water

•   Some chamomile, sage, and basil (herbs that are associated with prosperity)

•   1 dish of earth or salt

•   1 wand or athame

How to do it:

Cast the circle in whatever way you prefer.

Invite the god and goddess of prosperity to come to your circle. Use any method that you feel comfortable with such as a chant.

Visualize your objective. This may be money to pay off your bills or any purpose that would require you to have extra money. As you do this, toss the herbs into the burning charcoal.

Sprinkle some salt and several drops of water on the charcoal. Move your athame over the cauldron in a clockwise direction. This will help blend the energies together.

Then, say the following words:

By the powers of the elements of earth, wind, fire, and air

I cast this spell.

I ask the Universe for guidance as I request for help on this day.

I intend no harm to anyone.

May this spell be done.

Meditate for a few minutes. Visualize that the smoke coming from the cauldron is bringing the energies from the circle to the Universe.

Thank the god and goddess for their help in your request.

Release the circle, then ground and center yourself. Expect the money you need soon.

Chapter 6: Magickal Cooking Spells

Food, in itself and on its own, is magickal. It doesn't need other things to manifest its inherent magickal properties. Now, you may ask how this is possible. Simple! Food is gift from our Mother Earth.

Each life form in our planet is a miracle, and that is what food is – a miracle! All the herbs, veggies, and fruits that we eat are living plants, and are thus imbued with nourishment and love from Mother Earth.

Likewise, the meats and dairy we consume on a regular basis come from nature's amazing creatures. We should therefore treat them with gratitude and respect, as well.

You can easily prepare magickal meals just praying as you prepare them, as well as showing gratitude for the sustenance they provide. It is also important to remember that when you prepare a meal, any kind of energy that surrounds you has an effect on your food. So, when you feel happy as you work in the kitchen, singing and dancing while cooking, your meal will absorb the positive energy.

Mindfulness is a key part of cooking like a true Wiccan witch. This includes being mindful of all the ingredients you use, their properties, their history, and how they can sustain and nurture your body.

Having said that, the following sections will cover the different types of food you use in your kitchen in general, and in casting spells. These include some of the herbs discussed in a previous chapter, but on a different topic.

Magickal Veggies

-Carrot – Ruled by Mars, the root plant is associated with fertility and lust – because of its phallic shape! Many childless women eat carrots to encourage pregnancy. The plant's flower is called Queen Anne's Lace. It comes in different colors including orange, white and purple.

-Lettuce – Ruled by the moon, lettuce is associated with the water element. This is because it is mostly made up of water. Eat lettuce if you want to avoid getting sea-sick. You can also use it to cast protection spells. It is especially helpful when grown in your own garden as it will provide protection for your home.

Rubbing lettuce on your face or forehead will help you fall asleep fast. You can also use the vegetable for chastity and divination spells. It is a very healthy veggie to eat as it is rich in vitamins, fiber, and water content.

-Onion – Onion is one of the masculine root plants used in many forms of spells. You can cut it open and leave it in a room to absorb any lingering sickness. You can also grow it in your garden to provide protection for your home against all kinds of evil spirits. Onion is also a popular ingredient in lust and money spells. When placed under your pillow, it will induce prophetic dreams. Onion is part of the Holy Trinity of veggies that also includes celery and carrot.

-Potato – A staple in Irish households for centuries, potato was once believed to contain poison because it is a member of the nightshade family. It is now eaten in all parts of the globe. Potato is under the rule of the moon. When you eat potatoes fried or baked, you get relief from an upset stomach. It is also used in many healing spells.

-Zucchini – The vegetable that many think is a fruit, zucchini is ruled by the planet Jupiter. Raw, whole zucchini is often used for sex spells. To keep your husband or partner from cheating, just carve out his name on the vegetable, then freeze it. You can also eat the veggie for prosperity and protection.

Magickal Herbs

-Basil – The herb is a fixture in many Wiccan kitchens. It is a fragrant and useful herb often included in cooking, whether in fresh or dried form. Known as a lust herb, basil's aroma helps bring forth sexual energy.

-Bay – The herb's leaves have been used in Mediterranean cooking for centuries. When burned, bay helps enhance your psychic powers. To connect to different gods, add bay to different dishes such as those of Cuban, Greek, and Italian ethnicity.

-Chili Powder – Made from dried, ground chilis, chili powder has long been used in ancient folk magick. It is typically used for spells to "drive someone away" or "shut someone up." This spice boasts of a powerful kick. Thus, it should be carefully and wisely used in spells. Unless you prefer really spicy food, you must use it in moderate fashion in your food.

-Coriander/Colantro – The herb's seed is called coriander, while its leaf is called cilantro. Ruled by Mars, it is used for lust and love spells. If you wear the seeds, you will get relief from migraine headaches. The herb is great for chutney and salsa, and in flavoring different foods. It is also popular in healing spells.

-Cinnamon – The powdered root has many uses, including desserts and other dishes. Its magickal properties help in spells that involve money, abundance, love, and protection.

-Cumin – The ancient herb is ruled by Mars, and popular in Mediterranean and Middle Eastern cooking. It is often used to provide added flavor to meat dishes and stews. When blended into beverages, cumin promotes lust. You can also use it to provide love and protection.

-Oregano – Popular in Italian cooking as a flavoring for tomato and meat dishes. Ruled by Venus, oregano is used in spells for luck, happiness, and protection. It is also known to help enhance your psychic prowess.

-Peppermint – Invigorating and sweet-tasting, peppermint is often used in desserts. It can also be used as a tea. Carrying dried leaves of the herb in your wallet helps draw money to you. It can also relive stomach aches and sour stomachs. It brings good luck when grown in your own garden.

-Rosemary – The herb is often used to enhance psychic abilities and intuition. You can take it in supplement form to help improve your cognition and memory.

-Thyme – Ruled by Venus, the herb has a long association with fairies. It is used to purify and to draw pleasant dreams. It is also burned or worn to promote good health. You can use thyme in your food to invite love, courage, fortune, and psychic skill into your life.

Magickal Fruits, Sweets, Breads, and Condiments

-Apple – The fruit is the food that Wiccans consider sacred to the goddess and the Isle of Avalon. If you horizontally slice an apple through the center, you'll notice the star (w/ 5 points) formed by the fruit's seeds. Apples are often used in spells for love, garden magick, immortality, and healing.

-Banana – The everyday fruit is ruled by Mars. It keeps you away from accidents and harm as you travel by air or cross-country. If you want to improve your sexual endurance, dry and crush the fruit into powder form. Then, rub it all over your body. Bananas are blessed with potent lust properties due to their obvious phallic shape.

-Bagel – Round-shaped with a distinct hole, the bread is said to be ruled by Adonis. It comes in different types and flavors, and it is great for breakfast. Eating bagel helps create illusions. One warning, though. Never eat pork products with bagel as this will bring bad luck!

Sesame bagels are for prosperity. Poppy bagels are best consume before bedtime to improve dream activity. But, you should not consume it prior to taking a drug test as you will surely test positive for opiates because of the poppy seeds. Salt bagels help get rid of inconsistencies, while cinnamon bagels make giving flattery quite easy.

-Chocolate – You can use chocolate as a dessert in itself or as flavoring. You can also consume it as a beverage such as a hot chocolate or hot cocoa drink. Chocolate was consumed by Mayans and Aztecs because of the food's perceived ability to improve virility and power in the tribes' warriors.

Chocolate was sacred to many ancient cultures. It was considered as a power drug associated with intimacy and romance. Milk chocolate helps with friendships and nurturing. A staple ingredient for kitchen witches, chocolate is popular to those looking to induce love.

-Ketchup – Now, even common condiments possess magickal powers! Ruled by Venus, ketchup is made from tomatoes. If you want to dismiss or summon energy, draw a tomato-shaped pentagram. Spread ketchup on other foods to help you visualize friendships. Call out your target person's name while eating ketchup to develop friendship. The condiment is identified with love. This is because tomatoes were once believed to be potent aphrodisiacs.

-Orange – The fruit is famous the world over, and dates back to prehistoric times. It is often used in spells that involve joy, love, and inspiration. Place an orange in your Christmas stocking to encourage the sun to come back. The fruit is closely associated with solar magick and the sun itself. Eating oranges helps lift your spirits up. To use in abundance and love spells, just dry and grind oranges into powder form.

-Pasta – Mercury rules pasta. Spiral pasta improves creativity. Linguini/spaghetti provides protection, and helps improve communications. Corn pasta enhances financial creativity, and rice pasta promotes love.

-Pizza – The recreational and delicious food is under the sun's rule. Eat some pizza whenever things become difficult, and you badly need a lucky streak – or, anytime you get a craving for the comfort food.

-Rum – The alcoholic beverage is ruled by Chango and Ellegua. It channels the gods' spirits and it is used as an offering to win over the favor of the gods. Rum is used for baking rum cakes, among others. You can also use it for concocting wonderful cocktails or drink it on its own.

-Sugar – Ruled by Venus, the goddess of love, and by Orishas, sugar is a popular ingredient in spell bags, jars, and other charms. To draw your target's attention, sprinkle some sugar on red or pink love candles.

-Tomato – Many people think that tomato is a vegetable. It is not. In reality, it is a fruit. In Mediterranean countries, the tomato was considered as the fruit of love. It is a potent aphrodisiac that is commonly used in various Mexican, Greek, and Italian dishes.

-Salt – Salt has a lot of uses in baking and culinary arts. Mainly used as flavoring, it comes with cleansing and purifying effects. For centuries, it has been used to protect people and their homes from evil. It also helps absorb negative energies away. Salt comes in different varieties. Himalayan pink salt and sea salt are the best types to use for your body. Using "iodized table salt" is not a good idea.

Wiccan Magickal Cooking Spells

There are many magickal cooking spells for the kitchen Wiccan who prefers to toss in a bit of magick into the food they are preparing. Kitchen spells are an old form of magick that uses food and cooking as part of Wiccan rituals.

The spells not only provide some oomph to your meals. They will also help some of your wishes come true. They are also used to make everyday remedies and cures right in the home kitchen.

Kitchen spells are best done – of course – in a kitchen! But, you can always do it in the usual area where you cast your spells, such as your altar.

Bless Your Space

Although there are many general blessing spells that you can choose from to help bring magick into your kitchen, this spell is intended to specifically help you improve all the cooking you do in your kitchen.

What you'll need:

•   2 brown candles (if you can't find brown candles, the white variety will do)

•   2 sprigs of rosemary (fresh)

•   1 wooden spoon

•   1 wooden bowl

•   Your usual kitchen utensils

• Something powdery to represent your cooking style (you can use flour or other spies for this)

How to do it:

Place your candles at both ends of your counter, or anywhere you do a lot of cooking. Put a sprig of rosemary each in front of the candles. Place the bowl upside down right in the middle of the candles.

Light up the candles. Then, tap the wooden bowl four times. Sprinkle it with a dash of your powder. Then, say the spell words aloud:

Bless this kitchen where I cook

Show some magick wherever I look

Don't let anything burn

Don't let anything fall

Let my food be impressive to all.

Tap on the bowl once more. Sprinkle a few dashes of the powder you're using on the counter – from candle to candle. Tap another time, then say the spell words again. At this point, add some of the powder to each rosemary sprig.

Turn the bowl upright. Then, sprinkle a bit of additional powder in the bowl. Get the rosemary sprigs, then tie them up together. Lift the sprigs over the candle flames, making sure that they don't catch fire. This is done to give the candles more blessing.

Hang the sprigs from the door handle of a cabinet, or any other prominent place in your kitchen. Blow the powder or sweep it gently off the counter. Refrain from using water to wash it for a couple of hours or more. It is best to just leave everything as is, if possible.

Food Focus

If you have problems keeping up with recipe details, or it takes you a long time to manage the required food preparation and cooking steps, then this kitchen spell is for you! The spell involves keeping you focused on what you are doing. This way, you can properly do all the steps, detail by detail.

What you'll need:

- 1 coin

- 1 kitchen timer

- 1 piece of thread

How to do it:

Tie the piece of thread around your coin. Use a knot that will allow you to dangle the coin without disengaging it from the thread. Set your timer for 1 minute.

Dangle the coin right in front of your face. Focus your attention to the coin. Keep your eye on it at all times. You can blink, but never take your eyes away from the coin. Then, say the spell words fast, making sure that you finish before the timer runs out.

Mind on my task, is all I ask.

Once the timer sounds off, shut your eyes. Jerk the thread so you can catch the coin with your hand. Allow a minute to pass without doing anything, after which you can start cooking.

Prosperity Tea

A nice and warm cup of this herbal tea can help bring forth some extra boost to your financial life. An old kitchen spell recipe, the necessary herbs are all readily available in most household kitchens. If you prefer, you can even add a bit of honey to sweeten.

What you'll need:

- 1 pinch of fresh ginger (minced)

- 1 pinch of cinnamon (ground)

- 1 sprinkling of nutmeg (ground)

- 1 sprinkling of flax (ground)

How to do it:

Put a cup of water to a boil. Then, add all the herbal ingredients. Stir well, allowing the mixture to steep for about 10 minutes.

While the herbs steep, imagine your need for some extra money, and how more abundance can make your life a life a lot better. Then, say the following financial spell words:

A coin here, and a coin there

I see prosperity everywhere I look.

I need more wealth,

Financial wealth,

But I only want my fair share.

Use a strainer to remove the ginger bits and other herbs. If preferred, add some honey to sweeten. Make sure to consume the entire cup of prosperity tea before the brew gets cold.

Bless My Kitchen Charm

This is another herbal spell to bless your kitchen. This will help drive all negative energies away, and help you prepare your meals the best possible way!

What you'll need:

- 1 whole bay leaf

- 1 orange rind strip

- 1 length of string or rough twine

How to do it:

Tie the strip of orange rind and bay leaf to the rosemary's base. Wrap around several times to make sure everything is secure.

Hang the charm in a safe area in your kitchen. It will help purify your kitchen space, and deliver only positive energy to your household.

Conclusion

Congratulations! By reaching the conclusion, you must have absorbed so much knowledge and positive energy from this book. No longer are you a complete beginner in Wicca. Especially if you started to practice a few of the spells included in this guide.

But your journey should not end here. Nourish your passion towards Nature. Broaden your circles and meet fellow Wiccans. Understand and embrace your true self. The world of magick still has so much more in store for you.

If you've found "Wicca Spells" useful and would like to learn more about Wicca, I recommend you to please check my other book from the same series, "Wicca for Beginners".

CPSIA information can be obtained
at www.ICGtesting.com
Printed in the USA
LVHW011712100520
655310LV00016B/961

9 781950 855124